PARABLES OF KIERKEGAARD

PARABLES OF
KIERKEGAARD

Edited, with an Introduction, by
Thomas C. Oden

Illustrated by
Lonni Sue Johnson

PRINCETON UNIVERSITY PRESS

PRINCETON, NEW JERSEY

Library of Congress Cataloging-in-Publication Data

Kierkegaard, Søren, Aabye, 1813–1855.
Parables of Kierkegaard.

"Bibliography: Kierkegaard's works in
chronological order" : p.
Bibliography: p.
Includes index.
1. Parables. I. Oden, Thomas C. II. Title.
B4372.E5   1978   198'.9   78-51184
ISBN 0-691-07174-8
ISBN 0-691-02053-1 (pbk.)

First Princeton Paperback Printing, 1989

This book has been composed in Linotype Granjon

Princeton University Press books are printed on acid-free paper
and meet the guidelines for permanence and durability of the
Committee on Production Guidelines for Book Longevity
of the Council on Library Resources

Printed in the United States of America

10

Contents

Introduction

THE very word parable carries with it intriguing and memorable images in the history of western thought—of a good Samaritan, of a dark cave in which vague shadows dance on the wall (Plato), of a field mouse and a city mouse (Luther), of Bunyan's pilgrim, of Nietzsche's "ugliest man," Kafka's castle, Gide's Theseus, and John Hick's celestial travelers. There can be no doubt that the western philosophical tradition has turned perennially to parable as a means of communicating moral and spiritual insight.

No writer in that tradition has made more persistent use of parables, stories, and narrative metaphors than has Søren Kierkegaard (1813-1855), whose gift of storytelling has imprinted unforgettable images on our minds. The aim of this volume is to bring together a careful selection of these stories for edification, enjoyment, and critical examination. The essential conviction underlying this effort is that Kierkegaard ranks among the best of the great parabolists of the western tradition.

The mind of Kierkegaard has been kept alive in the common memory more by his parables than any other part of his authorship. Like all good parables, they have developed an oral tradition. Do not be surprised if you find here parables that you have heard imperfectly retold or partially revised. Now the reader can track down the original.

That these parables belong to the central tradition of western parable writing is commonly acknowledged. What is less well known is that Kierkegaard is one of the few writers in that tradition who was himself a literary critic, who himself offered a detailed theory of (indirect) communication that accounted for his writing in parable and story form under pseudonyms, and who clearly envisioned parabolic communication as an integral part of his philosophical method.

Kierkegaard's authorship is so vast and his method so complex that the ordinary reader is easily intimidated by it. Here, instead, we have a little book that anyone can read, that is not intimidating, yet reveals the central energies of his work as an author.

When we speak of Kierkegaard's parables, what in particular do we have in mind? Instead of answering abstractly, it is best to offer an example:

> There was a man whose chatter certain circumstances made it necessary for me to listen to. At every opportunity he was ready with a little philosophical lecture, a very tiresome harangue. Almost in despair, I suddenly discovered that he perspired copiously when talking. I saw the pearls of sweat gather on his brow, unite to form a stream, glide down his nose, and hang at the extreme point of his nose in a drop-shaped body. From the moment of making this discovery, all was changed. I even took pleasure in inciting him to begin his philosophical instruction, merely to observe the perspiration on his brow and at the end of his nose.[1]

This story is exemplary of Kierkegaard's parables, characterized as it is by an unexpected reversal, a condensed plot, and easy memorability for oral transmission. This parable in fact is a précis in story form of the whole essay on "the rotation method" in which it appears. Kierkegaard often caps off a longer essay by telling a story that nails down the point.

Because Kierkegaard's authorship is vast, searching for the hundreds of parables in his writing is like looking for veins of gold in a mountain. Having taught a seminar on Kierkegaard to graduate students for many years, I have witnessed this frequent dilemma: The reader will come across a beautiful

[1] *Either/Or* (hereafter *E/O*), I, p. 295.

parable embedded in the text, experience it powerfully, a month later remember it in vague outline, and two months later begin searching for it to no avail. The indices do not help. So the vein of gold remains hidden in the mountain. This repeated experience motivated me years ago to begin my own collection of parables that had particular significance for the study of Kierkegaard and for the edification of human experience. Thus a major motivation for this collection is the presentation of a well-indexed selection of his parables both for new and old readers and for literary and philosophical criticism.

Why do we read Kierkegaard's parables and why do they merit philosophical attention? Is it because they are like maddening puzzles daring some attempted solution? Is it because the problems they address drive to the depths of ordinary human experience? Or are they mere entertainment, revealing the comic side of human pretenses—subtle poetry, with virtually inexhaustible levels of meaning? Wherever the weight of the answer is to fall, anyone who lives with these parables for awhile experiences both their power and their beauty. Soon you realize that it is not you who are interpreting the parable but the parable that is interpreting you.

Storytelling was a preoccupation of Kierkegaard, whether in his private journals or edifying discourses or psychological experiments, or in the most closely reasoned philosophical dialect. What is less evident is *why* storytelling was so crucial to his whole authorship and intrinsic to his method of indirect communication. It can be said of Kierkegaard as it was said of Jesus, that "indeed he said nothing to them without a parable" (Matthew 13:34). Kierkegaard had a metaphoric mind. He communicated, and apparently thought, in dramaturgic images. One has the impression that it would have been impossible for him to communicate meaningfully in any other way, for it is difficult to find a long stretch of his writing where he does not take the reader aside and say: I will show you a picture of what I mean. He then presents the picture in

ix

the form of a brief story of spare characterization and surprising reversal, with the underlying intent of moral or spiritual illumination, which is precisely the classical definition of
a parable.

The use of parables served Kierkegaard's aims as an author
for at least five reasons, the first of which Kierkegaard himself
mentions as early as 1842, when he says that this approach
supplies him an excellent weapon in his philosophical-polemi-
cal arsenal. Using parables places his philosophical intentions
in stark contrast to the stilted, non-experiential Hegelian logic
against which he is struggling. In one of his earliest references
to his "method of story-telling," in *Johannes Climacus*, he
contrasts its simplicity with the labyrinthine confusions of
"modern philosophy":

> He who supposes that philosophy has never in the world
> been so near to solving its problem (which is the revealing
> of all secrets) as now, may well feel it odd, affected, offen-
> sive that I choose this method of story-telling, and do not,
> in my humble way, lend a hand with putting the coping-
> stone on the System. On the other hand, he who is con-
> vinced that philosophy has never been so perverted as
> now, so confused, in spite of all its definitions, so entirely
> to be likened to the weather last winter when we heard
> what had never been heard before, men crying mussels
> and prawns in such a way that he who attended to a par-
> ticular cry might at one time think it was winter, at an-
> other time spring, at another time midsummer; while he
> who paid attention to all these cries at once might think
> that Nature had become all muddled up, and the world
> could not continue till Easter—he will certainly think it
> right that I should try by means of this story-telling
> method, to counteract the abominable falsity which is the
> mark of modern philosophy; a philosophy which is speed-
> ily distinguished from older philosophy by its discovery
> of the ridiculousness of doing what one said one did or
> had done—he I say will find this story-telling method ap-

propriate, and will only be sorry, as I am, that the person who begins this task has not greater authority than I have.[2]

Like Socrates', Kierkegaard's philosophical quest was full of strife. So it is not surprising that he, like Socrates, so frequently elects to disarm his opponents with a seemingly innocuous story. "In its most characteristic use," wrote A. T. Cadoux, "the parable is a weapon of controversy, not shaped like a sonnet in undisturbed concentration, but improvised in conflict to meet an unpremeditated situation. And with this handicap it has at its best a delicacy and complexity of aptitudes showing a range of mind and genius of association beyond that required for the similes and metaphors of other poetic compositions."[3] It is with such aptitude and genius that Kierkegaard enlists the parable so effectively as a weapon of philosophical conflict.

A second reason why Kierkegaard turns so often to storytelling is that he quite evidently relishes meeting his reader in this way. He takes delight in leading his readers along a path, only to arrive at an unexpected junction where he suddenly leaves them to make a decision about a set of events. There is a play element in all good parable writing. Kierkegaard's view of play, however, is more akin to a fairly rough contact sport. "Literature should not be a nursing home for cripples," Kierkegaard wrote in 1843, "but a playground for healthy, happy, thriving, smiling, well-developed children of verve, finely formed, whole, satisfied beings, each one of whom is the very image of his mother and has his father's vitality— not the abortions of weak desires, not the refuse of afterbirth."[4]

What does the story format do for Kierkegaard's psychology and philosophy that could not be easily done by analytical discourse or direct, objective information? It disarms the reader,

[2] *Johannes Climacus or De omnibus dubitandum est, and A Sermon,* p. 102.
[3] A. T. Cadoux, *The Parables of Jesus,* p. 13.
[4] *Søren Kierkegaard's Journals and Papers* (hereafter *JP,* with *Papirer* entry reference in parenthesis), I, p. 57 (IV A 130).

putting him or her in a non-defensive, receptive frame of mind that allows the author to enter more deeply into personal communication with the reader. Kierkegaard found that a distinct advantage of parabolic communication is that it does not ask for any assent to systematic presuppositions or for any sacrifice of intellect, nor does it require commitment to any logical rules of procedure. It rather starts concretely with commonly experienced images presented benignly in the form of a narrative, allowing the readers to compare that story with their own perceptions. The readers are in a sense taken unawares into potentially new levels of insight when they identify vicariously first with the character who poses the dilemma and then with the developing circumstances of the plot that metaphorically bestows some unexpected angle of vision on the dilemma. So the readers often do not quite grasp what has hit them in this fantasized situation until they move more deeply into the self-examination that the parable elicits and requires. Thus, it should be remembered that, however witty these stories may be, Kierkegaard's purpose was not simply to amuse, but to edify, to upbuild (*opbygge*), to draw his readers into self-awareness, to sensitize moral and spiritual consciousness to the task and gift of authentic human existence.

This leads us to our third and most substantive reason why parabolic communication is so central to Kierkegaard's authorship: The story format was necessary for implementing his highly explicit theory and method of indirect communication, which was essential to the purpose of his writing. If *subjectivity* (or personal existence, or becoming oneself) *is truth*, which is Kierkegaard's premise ("the truth exists only in the process of becoming, in the process of appropriation"),[5] then the communication of truth must be quite different from the objective presentation of data or information. Such an "indirect" communication requires a "double reflection": on the one hand the communicator is imaginatively presenting alternative possibilities of self-understanding that call for decision

[5] *Concluding Unscientific Postscript* (hereafter *CUP*), p. 72.

xii

("either/or") by the reader; on the other hand the communicator is intensively concerned about what Kierkegaard calls "the appropriation process," that is, the means by which the reader grasps his or her own human possibilities.[6] "An example of such indirect communication is, so to compose jest and earnest that the composition is a dialectical knot—and with this to be nobody. If anyone is to profit by this sort of communication, he must himself undo the knot for himself."[7] This is exactly what the parables require of readers, that they untie the knot for themselves; and for this reason I deliberately make no attempt to write a standard or allegedly "correct" commentary on each parable, since each parable aims to challenge the subjective consciousness of the individual reader in its own way.

We have in Kierkegaard's writings (especially the *Journals and Papers, Concluding Unscientific Postscript, Training in Christianity*, and *The Point of View of My Work as an Author*) a detailed account of his own understanding of his indirect communication, along with an elaborate rationale for his use of pseudonyms. The parables clearly fall into Kierkegaard's category of indirect communication, because they confront us with a *choice* between possibilities of self-understanding, so that in the process of having to choose, we discover ourselves, or something of ourselves. Parable is indirect both because it tends to "deceive the hearer into the truth,"[8] and because it inconspicuously requires us to make imaginative choices, so that in doing so we are in some sense offered the possibility of more fully choosing to become ourselves.

That this task of indirect communication is exceedingly difficult is recognized by Kierkegaard in this analogy: "To stop a man on the street and stand still while talking to him, is not so difficult as to say something to a passer-by in passing, without standing still and without delaying the other, without

[6] *JP*, I, pp. 274ff (VIII² B 81).
[7] *Training in Christianity* (hereafter *TC*), pp. 132-33.
[8] *JP*, I, p. 288 (VIII² B 85).

xiii

attempting to persuade him to go the same way, but giving him instead an impulse to go precisely his own way. Such is the relation between one existing individual and another, when the communication concerns the truth as existential inwardness."[9]

The task of the parabolist is made even more difficult by the clear moral awareness that the ethical communicator is required "to *be* what he teaches!"[10] Furthermore, his personal address must be "as manifold as the opposites he holds in combination. . . . His form must first and last relate itself to existence, and in this connection he will have at his disposal the poetic, the ethical, the dialectical, and the religious."[11] This is why the parables of Kierkegaard are an interdisciplinary event. They must be broadly imaginative, yet narrowly focused in the service of the concrete, subjective existence of the hearer. Such an author "has only a single scene, existence, and he has nothing to do with beautiful valleys and the like. His scene is not the fairyland of the imagination, where the poet's love evokes the perfect; nor is the scene in England, and the task to make sure of local color and historical exactness. His scene is—inwardness in existing as a human being."[12]

Kierkegaard's parables aim not merely at a change of mind but a change of will. Kierkegaard does not tell his parables with the expectation that his hearers will experience a casual illumination or fascination, but rather that they might say to themselves, "Aha! I know how that is and it makes a difference in the way I understand myself and make fundamental choices!" If the parable is functioning maximally, "the spectators become participants, not because they want to necessarily, or simply have 'gotten the point,' but because they have, for the moment, 'lost control,' or as the new hermeneuts say, 'been interpreted.' "[13]

The fourth reason that parables served Kierkegaard's aims

[9] *CUP*, p. 247.   [10] *JP*, I, p. 287 (VIII² B 85).
[11] *CUP*, p. 319.   [12] *CUP*, pp. 319-20.
[13] Sallie Teselle, *Speaking in Parables*, p. 79.

follows as a consequence of the third. "All communcation of knowledge is direct communication," wrote Kierkegaard. "All communication of capability is indirect communication."[14] But what does Kierkegaard mean when he suggests that these stories intend to communicate a capability, rather than information? What kinds of capabilities do they communicate?

They communicate the capability of an altered vision of oneself that places the reader in an intensified internal self-relation. What Kierkegaard hoped from his parables is that they would draw or entice, even seduce in some instances, the individual into more profound extensions of self-awareness, and into a more fundamental affirmation of oneself as an unresolvable tension between possibility and necessity, finitude and infinitude, body and spirit.

Kierkegaard's parables intend to communicate an enriched capacity for self-examination leading to increased moral sensitivity and intensified spirituality. They offer his readers a potential gift, the acceptance of which requires their participation. A parable is not like an easily recognized object that is handed to someone to use, but like a gift that one first needs to open and then has to figure out what to do with it. The parables seek to facilitate a capability that can only be set in motion by the act of self-discovery, but that capability may remain dormant unless the self is jolted out of fixed behavioral routines, which the parables powerfully challenge.

A good parable, then, does not merely serve as an illustrative point, one that could easily be omitted from the text without being missed, but rather suddenly makes the larger intent of the text transparent. At the least it introduces new possibilities of self-understanding through its metaphor; at best it alters the consciousness of the reader.

Could Kierkegaard have accomplished such a change of consciousness without his parables and stories? It is doubtful. At least it is clear that in practice he constantly returns to them and in theory views indirect communication as a central re-

[14] *JP*, I, p. 282 (VIII B 83).

quirement of his authorship. Direct communication fails to communicate capability, even though it may succeed very well in communicating information. This is why the parables are pivotal for the whole of Kierkegaard's effort, because they seek to communicate to readers their own capacity to reach into their own experience with heightened self-awareness, to challenge them to come alive, to become themselves, to become persons, individuals in the richest sense. So the parables seek intensely to actualize what the whole authorship is after: to facilitate the birth of selfhood.

However, can these stories stand on their own as literature, or are they so deeply enmeshed in their context that they intrinsically resist anthologizing? The answer to this question leads us directly into the fifth reason why the parables deserve special attention: they are by the author's intention designed to serve oral tradition, and therefore in some measure they are able to stand alone as credible, and even astonishingly beautiful, literary entities.

In order to qualify as a parable in a literary sense, a story must have aesthetic balance, some trenchant elements of metaphorical imagination, brevity and economy, limited development of characterization, and a concentrated plot with a powerful "twist" or reversal of insight. In addition to fulfilling these criteria, a parable has to undergo some intergenerational testing, that is, must survive in the living memory of at least two or three generations.

On what grounds, then, do we argue that Kierkegaard's parables may be viewed as separable entitles and brought into a general collection? The answer must be offered basically on generic and literary grounds. As a distinctive literary genre, the parable, by definition, is intended to be remembered, to lend itself to oral retelling. Memorability is thus a crucial criterion for any parable. Therefore an astute writer of parables has precisely in mind the detachability of the parable from its original context, otherwise his purpose is defeated. If, before telling or commenting upon the parable of the prodigal son, one were required to place it in its original historical context, the parable would seldom be told or remembered. But, it has been remembered, and it has been appropriated in and out of many historical contexts, often in ignorance of its original context. I am not hereby approving of historical ignorance vis-à-vis parables, and, in fact, this collection of Kierkegaard's parables provides biographical information and interpretive assistance to the reader in notes where necessary, particularly in the case of several enigmatic parables. But most of the parables can stand alone, and do.

This memorability criterion has been an influential standard for this selection. Out of many hundreds of parables I have selected only a few, and avid Kierkegaard readers will wish that many more could have been included. (For them a list of omitted parables appears as an appendix, with English and Danish text references.) But the parables included here are those, in my judgment, most worthy of remembering and telling, with good reversal, rich imagery, and concise thematic development. For parables are distinguished from novels or short shories precisely at this point: they direct themselves particularly to memory, oral repetition, and adaptation.

I have set forth five reasons why these parables play such a crucial role in Kierkegaard's authorship: they serve as valuable polemical weapons for combat with the philosophical assumptions of his day; Kierkegaard has an unremitting love, and an extraordinary gift, for story-telling that manifests itself in every aspect of his multifaceted career as a writer; the story format is necessary for implementing his highly explicit method of indirect communication, which he regards as a central feature of his entire authorship; through the parables he seeks to actualize what the whole authorship is after, to facilitate the birth of selfhood; and of all his many different kinds of writing, the parables lend themselves most easily to memory and oral repetition.

But do these stories indeed refract the central beam of light of Kierkegaard's authorship? This will be debated by scholars and critics. Rather than attempting to settle the issue, the most this volume can do is offer a better frame of reference for its pursuit by gathering for the first time some of the parables in a single collection for critical examination as well as for enjoyment and instruction. My own opinion is that these parables for the most part stand on their own as enduring literary gems, explosive multicolored bursts of moral and spiritual illumination on the darkened skies of modernity, intriguing puzzles that invite the ordinary reader's most intense reflection and extended contemplation. They do not need a committee of experts to provide an elaborate apparatus of interpretation or historical excursi or hints for allegorization. They only need you, the reader, to read them, preferably aloud ("My dear reader: If it be possible, read aloud!"),[15] yet in the silence of deepening interiority.

[15] For *Self-Examination* and *Judge for Yourselves!* and *Three Discourses*, p. 29.

Acknowledgments and Notes

IN presenting these parables, I wish to express special gratitude to W.B.J. Martin, who conceived the idea of this collection with me in 1959; to the Arthur Vining Davis Foundation, the Lilly Foundation, and the Association of Theological Schools, who provided supportive grants for this project; to the University of Texas and the Austin Presbyterian Theological Seminary for many resources extended to facilitate its accomplishment; to Clayton Meyer, Randall Berkey, and Lloyd Parrill for valuable research assistance; to Dean Bard Thompson and Dean James E. Kirby of Drew University for their constant encouragement; to the many bright students in my Kierkegaard seminars at Drew, and the seminaries at Princeton, Claremont, and Phillips; and above all to my principal mentors in Kierkegaard studies, the late H. Richard Niebuhr of Yale and the late Will Herberg of Drew.

I express special thanks to the Princeton University Press not only for their wise counsel in the development of this project, grounded in their long term interest in Kierkegaard in English translation, but also for allowing me a certain editorial freedom to make modest stylistic revisions [in brackets] in the translations, and in the case of certain parables to change Walter Lowrie's translation of "Du" from "thee" to "you," and to modernize usages like "wouldst."

The following parables are used by permission of the Augsburg Publishing House: The Silenced Petition, Solomon's Dream, The Storm, The Untouched Food, and The Diagnosis. The parables entitled Boredom, The Wager, The Jewel on Thin Ice, The Swindler and the Widow's Mite, The Button, The August Holiday, and The Imagined Rebellion are by permission of Oxford University Press. The Confessor and the Penitent, The Self-assured Policeman, The Interrupted

Wise Man, The Two Artists, The Costume of the Actor, The Man Who Walked Backwards, The Prompter, The Dangerous Instrument, and The Needlewoman are by permission of Harper and Row and William Collins & Co., Ltd. The parable in the Introduction, p. x, is by permission of A. & C. Black, Ltd. The remainder of the parables are by permission of Princeton University Press.

With the exception of two parables, all parables in this collection are from English translations of Kierkegaard's *Samlede Vaerker* (hereafter *SV*), the preferred English translations being indicated in the Bibliography. Copious parabolic materials from the *Papirer*, although excellent in quality in many cases, were not included in this selection on the grounds that (a) they would be so extensive as to justify separate treatment, perhaps in a subsequent volume, and (b) they were written, for the most part, not for publication, but as parts of a private journal or recollection, and thus constitute a distinguishable type of writing requiring special treatment beyond the range and space limitations of this volume.

The parable title and the lead question that introduce each parable in this collection are not found directly in the text but are in most cases unmistakably derived from the text or its context. They will assist the reader in locating quickly the issue or dilemma to which the parable speaks as a metaphorical response. The format I have chosen bears certain similarities to the tradition of the rabbinic *mashalim*, which focus on a single theme, begin with a dilemma or paradox, and are referred to by definite titles.

In this edition, following Hong and Hong's format in *Søren Kierkegaard's Journals and Papers*, a series of five periods (. . . . .) indicates a break or pause point (sometimes a dash or colon) found in the Danish text and in the English translation, whereas three dots (. . .) indicates an omission I have made in editing the text to eliminate excursi or extraneous materials.

Finally, I have scrupulously honored Kierkegaard's specific

request in *Concluding Unscientific Postscript*, "A First and Last Declaration," that "if it might occur to anyone to quote a particular saying from the [pseudonymous] books, he would do me the favor to cite the name of the respective pseudonymous author. . . ."

Abbreviations

AC	*Attack Upon "Christendom"*
CD	*Christian Discourses*
COD	*Concept of Dread*
CUP	*Concluding Unscientific Postscript*
E/O	*Either/Or*
FT	*Fear and Trembling*
JP	*Søren Kierkegaard's Journals and Papers*
PF	*Philosophical Fragments*
SLW	*Stages on Life's Way*
SV	*Samlede Vaerker*
TC	*Training in Christianity*

List of the Parables

PARABLES OF KIERKEGAARD

The Happy Conflagration

What happens to those who try to warn the present age?

It happened that a fire broke out backstage in a theater. The clown came out to inform the public. They thought it was just a jest and applauded. He repeated his warning, they shouted even louder. So I think the world will come to an end amid general applause from all the wits, who believe that it is a joke.

"A" in Either/Or, I, p. 30 (SV II 30)

The Victims of Phalaris

What is a poet?

What is a poet? An unhappy man who in his heart harbors a deep anguish, but whose lips are so fashioned that the moans and cries which pass over them are transformed into ravishing music. His fate is like that of the unfortunate victims whom the tyrant Phalaris[1] imprisoned in a brazen bull, and slowly tortured over a steady fire; their cries could not reach the tyrant's ears so as to strike terror into his heart; when they reached his ears they sounded like sweet music. And men crowd about the poet and say to him, "Sing for us soon again"—which is as much as to say, "May new sufferings torment your soul, but may your lips be fashioned as before; for the cries would only distress us, but the music, the music, is delightful." And the critics come forward and say, "That is perfectly done—just as it should be, according to the rules of aesthetics." Now it is understood that a critic resembles a poet to a hair; he only lacks the anguish in his heart and the music upon his lips. I tell you, I would rather be a swineherd, understood by the swine, than a poet misunderstood by men.

"A" in *Either/Or*, I, p. 19 (*SV* II 23)

4

The Busy Philosopher

*What is left for the philosopher to do when
a society is preparing for war?*

When Philip threatened to lay siege to the city of Corinth,
and all its inhabitants hastily bestirred themselves in defense,
some polishing weapons, some gathering stones, some repair-
ing the walls, Diogenes seeing all this hurriedly folded his
mantle about him and began to roll his tub zealously back and
forth through the streets. When he was asked why he did this
he replied that he wished to be busy like all the rest, and
rolled his tub lest he should be the only idler among so many
industrious citizens.[2]

Johannes Climacus in *Philosophical Fragments*, p. 4
(*SV* VI 9-10)

Sulphur-Match Authors

*To what shall we compare the journalistic opinion-
peddlers who have an instant viewpoint on everything?*

. . . They may best be likened to sulphur-matches which are
sold in bundles. Such an author, upon whose head is deposited
something phosphorescent (the suggestion of a project, a
hint), one takes up by the legs and strikes him upon a news-
paper, and out there come three to four columns. And the
premise-authors have really a striking resemblance to sulphur-
matches—both explode with a puff.

On Authority and Revelation, pp. 5-6 (*Pap.* VII B 235)

The Author Who Could Not Write Fast Enough

Excessive self-confidence—how is it challenged?

A man . . . several years ago honored me with his literary confidence. He came to me lamenting that he was to such a degree overwhelmed by fullness of ideas that it was impossible for him to put down anything on paper, because he could not write fast enough. He begged me to be so kind as to be his secretary and write at his dictation. I at once smelled a rat and promptly consoled him with the assurance that I could write as fast as a runaway horse, since I wrote only a letter of each word and yet guaranteed that I could read everything I had written. My willingness to be of service knew no bounds. I had a big table brought out, numbered many sheets of paper, in order that I might not even waste time in turning a page, laid out a dozen steel pens with their holders, dipped my pen—and the man began his address as follows: "Well, yes, you see, my dear Sir, what I really wanted to say was . . . . ." When he was through with the address I read it aloud to him, and from that time he has never asked me to be his secretary.

Constantine Constantius in *Repetition*, pp. 60-61 (*SV* V 144)

6

The French Statesman

Can we have power without responsibility?

It is still fresh in our memory that a French statesman,[3] when a portfolio was offered to him for a second time, declared that he would accept it, but only on the condition that the secretary of state be made responsible. It is well known that the king of France is not responsible, while his minister is; the minister does not wish to be responsible, but will be minister with the proviso that the secretary of state become responsible; naturally, the final result is that the watchmen or street commissioners become responsible. Would not this story of shifted responsibility really be a proper subject for Aristophanes!

"A" in *Either/Or*, I, p. 140 (*SV* I 131-32)

7

The Vicious Dog

What is "the public"?

If I tried to imagine the public as a particular person . . . I should perhaps think of one of the Roman emperors, a large well-fed figure, suffering from boredom, looking only for the sensual intoxication of laughter, since the divine gift of wit is not earthly enough. And so for a change he wanders about, indolent rather than bad, but with a negative desire to dominate. Every one who has read the classical authors knows how many things a Caesar could try out in order to kill time. In the same way the public keeps a dog to amuse it. That dog is the sum of the literary world. If there is some one superior to the rest, perhaps even a great man, the dog is set on him and the fun begins. The dog goes for him, snapping and tearing at his coattails, allowing itself every possible ill-mannered familiarity—until the public tires, and says it may stop. That is an example of how the public levels. Their betters and superiors in strength are mishandled—and the dog remains a dog which even the public despises. The levelling is therefore done by a third party; a non-existent public levelling with the help of a third party which in its insignificance is less than nothing, being already more than levelled. . . . The public is unrepentant, for it is not they who own the dog—they only subscribe. They neither set the dog on any one, nor whistle it off—directly. If asked they would answer: the dog is not mine, it has no master. And if the dog had to be killed they would say: it was really a good thing that bad-tempered dog was put down, every one wanted it killed—even the subscribers.

The Present Age, pp. 65-66 *(SV* XIV 86-87)

8

A Permit for Prostitution

What is comedy?

When a woman seeks permission to establish herself as a public prostitute, this is comical. We properly feel that it is difficult to become something respectable (so that when a man is refused permission to become master of the hounds, for example, this is not comical), but to be refused permission to become something despicable, is a contradiction. To be sure, if she receives permission, it is also comical, but the contradiction is different, namely, that the legal authority shows its impotence precisely when it shows its power: its power by giving permission, its impotence by not being able to make it permissible.[4]

Johannes Climacus in *Concluding Unscientific Postscript*, p. 460n (*SV* X 191n)

The Endless Parade

To what shall we compare the inexhaustibility of reflection?

It is like Tordenskjold with his famous parade:[5] it uses over and over again the same few troops, but when they have marched past the reviewing stand they turn into a side street, don another uniform, and thus continue the parade . . . . . of the incalculable forces of the garrison.

Quidam in *Stages on Life's Way*, p. 227 (*SV* VIII 59)

9

The Costly Book Purchase

If conscience is circumvented, does it finally take its toll?

[It is] like the woman who offered to sell to Tarquin a collection of books and when he would not give the sum she demanded burned one-third of them and demanded the same sum, and when again he would not give the sum she demanded burned another third of them and demanded the same sum, until finally he gave the original sum for the last third.

Judge William in *Either/Or*, II, p. 213 (*SV* III 194)

The Pilgrim

To what shall we compare a decisive commitment that proceeds on an erroneous basis?

If a pilgrim who had wandered for ten years, taking two steps forward and one step backwards, if now he were to see the Holy City in the distance and he was [finally][6] told that this was not the Holy City—oh, well, he would walk farther— but if he was told, "This is the Holy City, but your way of progressing is entirely wrong, you must wean yourself from this way of walking if you would be well-pleasing to heaven!" He who for ten years had walked thus with the utmost exertion!

Quidam in *Stages on Life's Way*, pp. 211-12 (*SV* VIII 43)

The Boredom of the Gods

Is boredom a perennial human condition?

The gods were bored, and so they created man. Adam was bored because he was alone, and so Eve was created. [From that moment on]⁷ boredom entered the world, and increased in proportion to the increase of population. Adam was bored alone; then Adam and Eve were bored together; then Adam and Eve and Cain and Abel were bored *en famille*; then the population of the world increased, and the peoples were bored *en masse*. To divert themselves they conceived the idea of constructing a tower high enough to reach the heavens. This idea is itself as boring as the tower was high, and constitutes a terrible proof of how boredom gained the upper hand. . . . I desire no disciples; but if there happened to be someone present at my deathbed, and I was sure that the end had come, then I might in an attack of philanthropic delirium, whisper my theory in his ear, uncertain whether I had done him a service or not.⁸

"A" in *Either/Or*, I, pp. 282-84 (*SV* II 264-66)

The Silenced Petition

Is prayer hazardous?

An ancient pagan, who in pagandom was renowned and praised for his wisdom, sailed on the same ship with a wicked man. When the ship was in distress the wicked man lifted up his voice in prayer, but the wise man said to him: "Keep quiet, my friend; if heaven discovers that you are on board, the ship will go under."

Edifying Discourses, I, p. 74 (*SV* IV 58)

The Critical Apparatus

What is the difference between criticism of a text and radical accountability to it?

Imagine a country. A royal command is issued to all the office-bearers and subjects, in short, to the whole population. A remarkable change comes over them all: they all become interpreters, the office-bearers become authors, every blessed day there comes out an interpretation more learned than the last, more acute, more elegant, more profound, more ingenious, more wonderful, more charming, and more wonderfully charming. Criticism which ought to survey the whole can hardly attain survey of this prodigious literature, indeed criticism itself has become a literature so prolix that it is impossible to attain a survey of the criticism. Everything became interpretation—but no one read the royal command with a view to acting in accordance with it. And it was not only that everything became interpretation, but at the same time the point of view for determining what seriousness is was altered, and to be busy about interpretation became real seriousness. Suppose that this king was not a human king—for though a human king would understand well enough that they were making a fool of him by giving the affair this turn, yet as a human king he is dependent, especially when he encounters the united front of office-bearers and subjects, and so would be compelled to put the best face on a bad game, to let it seem as if all this were a matter of course, so that the most elegant interpreter would be rewarded by elevation to the peerage, the most acute would be knighted, &c.—Suppose that this king was almighty, one therefore who is not put to embarrassment though all the office-bearers and all the subjects play him false. What do you suppose this almighty king would think about such a thing? Surely he would say, "The fact that they do not comply with the commandment, even that I might forgive; moreover, if they united in a petition that I might have patience with them, or perhaps relieve them entirely of this commandment which seemed to them too hard—that I could forgive them. But this I cannot forgive, that they entirely alter the point of view for determining what seriousness is."[9]

For Self-Examination, pp. 58-59 (*SV* XVII 69-73)

13

The Refurbished Guidebook

*What level of understanding of the New Testament
has been achieved by modernity?*

The New Testament . . . regarded as a guide for Christians,
becomes, under the assumption we have made, a historical
curiosity, pretty much like a guidebook to a particular country
when everything in that country has been totally changed.
Such a guidebook serves no longer the serious purpose of being
useful to travelers in that country, but at the most it is worth
reading for amusement. While one is making the journey
easily by railway, one reads in the guidebook, "Here is Woolf's
Gullet where one plunges 70,000 fathoms down under the
earth"; while one sits and smokes one's cigar in the snug café,
one reads in the guidebook, "Here it is a band of robbers has
its stronghold, from which it issues to assault the travelers and
maltreat them"; here it is, etc. Here it is; that is, here it *was*;
for now (it is very amusing to imagine how it was), now
there is no Woolf's Gullet but the railway, and no robber
band, but a snug café.

Attack Upon "Christendom," p. 111 *(SV XIX 123)*

14

The Wager

*How much moral and spiritual vitality remains
in the "heroics of modernity"?*

It is said that two English noblemen were once riding along a
road when they met a man whose horse had run away with
him and who, being in danger of falling off, shouted for help.
One of the Englishmen turned to the other and said, "A hundred guineas he falls off." "Taken," said the other. With that
they spurred their horses to a gallop and hurried on ahead to
open the tollgates and to prevent anything from getting in the
way of the runaway horse. In the same way, though without
that heroic and millionaire-like spleen, our own reflective and
sensible age is like a curious, critical and worldly-wise person
who, at the most, has vitality enough to lay a wager.

The Present Age, p. 78 (*SV* XIV 94)

The Jewel on Thin Ice

*What is the difference between an engaged, passionate age
and the objective spectatorship of modernity?*

If the jewel which every one desired to possess lay far out on a
frozen lake where the ice was very thin, watched over by the
danger of death, while, closer in, the ice was perfectly safe,
then in a passionate age the crowds would applaud the courage
of the man who ventured out, they would tremble for him and
with him in the danger of his decisive action, they would
grieve over him if he were drowned, they would make a god
of him if he secured the prize. But in an age without passion,
in a reflective age, it would be otherwise. People would think

15

each other clever in agreeing that it was unreasonable and not even worth while to venture so far out. And in this way they would transform *daring and enthusiasm* into a *feat of skill,* so as to do something, for after all "something must be done." The crowds would go out to watch from a safe place, and with the eyes of connoisseurs appraise the accomplished skater who could skate almost to the very edge (i.e. as far as the ice was still safe and the danger had not yet begun) and then turn back. The most accomplished skater would manage to go out to the furthermost point and then perform a still more dangerous-looking run, so as to make the spectators hold their breath and say: "Ye Gods! How mad; he is risking his life."

The Present Age, pp. 37-38 (*SV* XIV 66-67)

The Knight's Choice

*To what shall we compare the irrevocability of
an "either/or" decision?*

. . . Suppose two opposing armies drawn up in the field, and that a knight arrives whom both armies invite to fight on their side; he makes his choice, is vanquished and taken prisoner. As prisoner he is brought before the victor, to whom he foolishly presumes to offer his services on the same terms as were extended to him before the battle. Would not the victor say to him: My friend, you are now my prisoner; there was indeed a time when you could have chosen differently, but now everything is changed. . . . "One who throws a stone has power over it until he has thrown it, but not afterwards" (Aristotle).[10] Otherwise throwing would be an illusion; the thrower would keep the stone in his hand in spite of all his throwing. . . .

Johannes Climacus in *Philosophical Fragments*,
pp. 20n-21n (*SV* VI 20n-21n)

The Lost Lover

Does despair consume itself?

A young girl is in despair over love, and so she despairs over her lover, because he died, or because he was unfaithful to her. This is not a declared despair; no, she is in despair over herself. This self of hers, which, if it had become "his" beloved, she would have been rid of in the most blissful way, or would have lost, this self is now a torment to her when it has to be a self without "him"; this self which would have been to her her riches (though in another sense equally in despair) has now become to her a loathsome void, since "he" is dead, or it has become to her an abhorrence, since it reminds her of the fact that she was betrayed. Try it now, say to such a girl, "You are consuming yourself," and you shall hear her reply, "Oh, no, the torment is precisely this, that I cannot do it."

To despair over oneself, in despair to will to be rid of oneself, is the formula for all despair.

Anti-Climacus in *The Sickness unto Death*,
pp. 152-53 (*SV* XV 79)

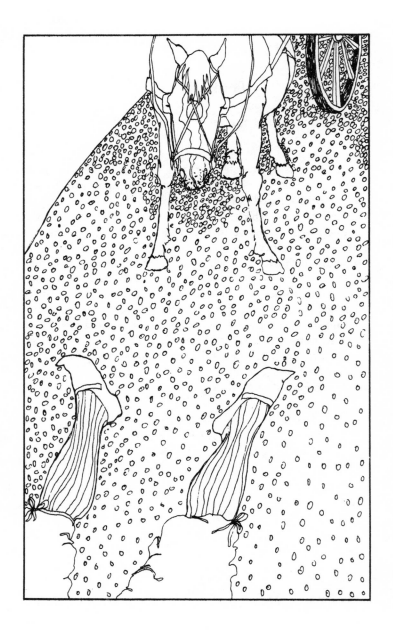

18

The New Shoes

When the task is becoming oneself, to what shall we compare the individual who does not even recognize that he has, or is, a self?

It is related of a peasant who came [barefooted][11] to the Capital, and had made so much money that he could buy himself a pair of shoes and stockings and still had enough left over to get drunk on—it is related that as he was trying in his drunken state to find his way home he lay down in the middle of the highway and fell asleep. Then along came a wagon, and the driver shouted to him to move or he would run over his legs. Then the drunken peasant awoke, looked at his legs, and since by reason of the shoes and stockings he didn't recognize them, he said to the driver, "Drive on, they are not my legs."

Anti-Climacus in *The Sickness unto Death*,
p. 187 (*SV* XV 109-10)

The Laughter of Parmeniscus

What is the laughter of disenchantment?

As it befell Parmeniscus in the legend,[12] who in the cave of Trophonius lost the power to laugh, but got it again on the island of Delos, at the sight of the shapeless block exhibited there as the image of the goddess Leto, so it has befallen me. When I was young, I forgot how to laugh in the cave of Trophonius; when I was older, I opened my eyes and beheld reality, at which I began to laugh, and since then I have not stopped laughing. I saw that the meaning of life was to secure a livelihood, and that its goal was to attain a high position; that love's rich dream was marriage with an heiress; that friendship's blessing was help in financial difficulties; that wisdom was what the majority assumed it to be; that enthusiasm consisted in making a speech; that it was courage to risk the loss of ten dollars; that kindness consisted in saying, "You are welcome," at the dinner table; that piety consisted in going to communion once a year. This I saw, and I laughed.

"A" in *Either/Or*, I, p. 33 (*SV* II 36)

20

The Dog Kennel by the Palace

To what shall we compare the relation between the
thinker's system and his actual existence?

A thinker erects an immense building, a system, a system
which embraces the whole of existence and world-history etc.
—and if we contemplate his personal life, we discover to our
astonishment this terrible and ludicrous fact, that he himself
personally does not live in this immense high-vaulted palace,
but in a barn alongside of it, or in a dog kennel, or at the most
in the porter's lodge. If one were to take the liberty of calling
his attention to this by a single word, he would be offended.
For he has no fear of being under a delusion, if only he can get
the system completed . . . . . by means of the delusion.

Anti-Climacus in *The Sickness unto Death*,
pp. 176-77 (*SV* XV 100)

The Decorative Copybook

How do the masses judge extraordinariness?

Suppose that an author who neither has a significant fund of
ideas nor is very hard-working should once in a great while
publish a decorative copybook, very dainty and elegantly put
together, with many blank pages: then the masses would look
upon this decorative phenomenon with wonder and admiration. They would think: since it has taken him so long to write

21

it, and since there is so little written on the pages, it must be something really extraordinary. Suppose on the other hand that a highly productive author, who has other things to think about than being decorative and profiting from a deception, should by exerting himself with greater and greater diligence find himself able to work with exceptional speed. The masses would soon get used to that, and would think: it must be a careless job. . . . Suppose there were a pastor, who like the late Chaplain-to-the-Court in Berlin, the otherwise so highly gifted Theremin[13] preached only every eighth Sunday or even just every twelfth, but who did so in the most regal and exalted presence of Their Majesties and the whole royal household: a deception would therefore immediately develop about such a Head-Chaplain-to-the-Court. He becomes—well, in truth he of course remains what he really is, a highly gifted man. But in the eyes of the masses he becomes not only the Head-Chaplain-to-the-Court but a Right Reverend Sir besides, or a Right Ruffled Head-Chaplain-to-the-Court, something Right Resplendent, like the king's golden coach, which one beholds with awe only a few times a year. The masses will be deeply impressed, and in their wisdom they will reflect as follows: such a preacher needs three months just to prepare one sermon and memorize it, so it must be extraordinary. And behold, the crowd of curiosity-seekers is so great on the long-awaited eighth or twelfth Sunday that the Head-Chaplain-to-the-Court is scarcely able to squeeze up into the pulpit—had he preached only once a year, the crowd would have been so huge that he would not have been able to squeeze down again at all, or policemen and armed sextons would have been needed to secure the Right Reverend Head-Chaplain's going out and coming in. And if the crowd were so great that someone were squeezed and trampled to death, then the next time the crowd would be still greater. For the dictum holds with regard not only to the truth, but also to curiosity: *"Sanguis martyrum est semen ecclesiae."*[14]

Crisis in the Life of an Actress, pp. 82-83 (*SV* XIV 117-18)

The Tyrant-Historian

*What is the value of objective historical research
for faith's decision?*

. . . Suppose we try to estimate the value of this relative difference, that which marks the first generation of secondary
disciples over against later ones; how great a value shall we
assign to it? We can evaluate it only by comparing it with the
advantage enjoyed by a contemporary. But his advantage, the
advantage namely of immediate certainty in the strict sense,
we have already shown . . . to be ambiguous (*anceps*—dangerous), and we shall show this further in the next paragraph.

—Suppose there lived a man in the immediately succeeding
generation[15] who combined in his own person a tyrant's
power with a tyrant's passion, and suppose that this man had
somehow conceived the idea of concentrating his entire time
and energy upon the problem of bringing the truth to light on
this point, would this constitute him a disciple? Suppose he
possessed himself of all the contemporary witnesses still living,
together with the immediate circle of their associates; suppose
he subjected them one by one to the most searching inquisition,
shutting them up in prison like the seventy interpreters,[16]
starving them to make them tell the truth, confronting them
with one another in the craftiest possible manner, all for the
sake of making sure by every possible means of a reliable account—would the possession of this account constitute him a
disciple? Must not the God[17] rather smile at him, because he
thought to arrogate to himself in this manner what cannot be
purchased for money, nor yet seized by violence? Even if the
fact we speak of were a simple historical fact, difficulties
would not fail to present themselves as soon as he tried to
realize an absolute agreement in all petty details, which would

be of extreme importance to him, because the passion of faith, i.e., the passion with the intensity of faith, had been misdirected upon the merely historical as its object. It is a familiar fact that the most conscientious and truthful of witnesses are the first to involve themselves in contradiction when subjected to inquisitorial treatment and questioned in the light of an inquisitor's fixed idea; while it is the prerogative of a hardened criminal, on account of the precision which an evil conscience tends to enforce, not to contradict himself in his lie. But leaving this aside, the fact of which we speak is not a simple historical fact: of what advantage then is all this precision?[18] If he succeeded in bringing to pass a complicated account, consistent to the letter and to the minute, he would beyond all doubt be deceived. He would have obtained a certainty even greater than was possible for a contemporary observer, one who saw and heard; for the latter would quickly discover that he sometimes failed to see what was there, and sometimes saw what was not there, and so with his hearing. And besides, a contemporary would constantly be reminded that he did not see or hear the God immediately, but merely a humble human being. . . .

Johannes Climacus in *Philosophical Fragments*,
pp. 114-16 (*SV* VI 83-84)

Solomon's Dream

*When despair intensifies, how may it affect
the whole of one's existence?*

Solomon's judgment is well enough known, it availed to
discriminate between truth and deceit and to make the judge
famous as a wise prince. His dream is not so well known.

If there is any pang of sympathy, it is that of having to be
ashamed of one's father, of him whom one loves above all and
to whom one is most indebted, to have to approach him backwards, with averted face, in order not to behold his dishonor.
But what greater bliss of sympathy can be imagined than to
dare to love as the son's wish prompts, and in addition to dare
to be proud of him because he is the only elect, the singularly
distinguished man, a nation's strength, a country's pride, God's
friend, a promise for the future, extolled in his lifetime, held
by memory in the highest praise! Happy Solomon, this was
thy lot! Among the chosen people (how glorious even to belong to them!) he was the King's son (enviable lot!), son of
that king who was the elect among kings!

Thus Solomon lived happily with the prophet Nathan. The
father's strength and the father's achievement did not inspire
him to deeds of valor, for in fact no occasion was left for that,
but it inspired him to admiration, and admiration made him a
poet. But if the poet was almost jealous of his hero, the son
was blissful in his devotion to the father.

Then the son one day made a visit to his royal father. In the
night he awoke at hearing movement where the father slept.
Horror seizes him, he fears it is a villain who would murder
David. He steals nearer—he beholds David with a crushed and
contrite heart, he hears a cry of despair from the soul of the
penitent.

Faint at the sight he returns to his couch, he falls asleep, but he does not rest, he dreams, he dreams that David is an ungodly man, rejected by God, that the royal majesty is the sign of God's wrath upon him, that he must wear the purple as a punishment, that he is condemned to rule, condemned to hear the people's benediction, whereas the Lord's righteousness secretly and hiddenly pronounces judgment upon the guilty one; and the dream suggests the surmise that God is not the God of the pious but of the ungodly, and that one must be an ungodly man to be God's elect—and the horror of the dream is this contradiction.

While David lay upon the ground with crushed and contrite heart, Solomon arose from his couch, but his understanding was crushed. Horror seized him when he thought of what it is to be God's elect. He surmised that holy intimacy with God, the sincerity of the pure man before the Lord, was not the explanation, but that a private guilt was the secret which explained everything.

And Solomon became wise, but he did not become a hero; and he became a thinker, but he did not become a man of prayer; and he became a preacher, but he did not become a believer; and he was able to help many, but he was not able to help himself; and he became sensual, but not repentant; and he became contrite and cast down, but not again erect, for the power of the will had been strained by that which surpassed the strength of the youth. And he tossed through life, tossed about by life—strong, supernaturally strong, that is, womanishly weak in the stirring infatuations and marvellous inventions of imagination, ingenious in expounding thoughts. But there was a rift in his nature, and Solomon was like the paralytic who is unable to support his own body. In his harem he sat like a disillusioned old man, until desire for pleasure awoke and he shouted, "Strike the timbrels, dance before me, ye women." But when the Queen of the South [sic][19] came to visit him, attracted by his wisdom, then was his soul rich, and the wise answer flowed from his lips like the precious myrrh which flows from the trees in Arabia.[20]

Quidam in *Stages on Life's Way*, pp. 236-37 (*SV* VIII 68-69)

The Dwarf's Seven-League Boots

Why is the pursuit of happiness so elusive?

Most men pursue pleasure with such breathless haste that they hurry past it. They fare as did that dwarf who kept guard over a captured princess in his castle. One day he took a midday nap. When he woke up an hour later, the princess was gone. Quickly he pulled on his seven-league boots; with one stride he was far beyond her.

"A" in *Either/Or*, I, p. 28 (*SV* II 31-32)

The Lonely Horse

To what shall we compare misunderstood suffering?

Let us assume that dumb animals could have thoughts and could make themselves understood to one another even though we could not make out what they said, let us take that for granted. It seems almost as if this were so. For when in summer the peasant's horse stands in the meadow and throws up his head or shakes it, surely no one can know with certainty what that means; or when two of them who throughout their lives have walked side by side pulling in the same yoke are turned out at night, when they approach one another as if in intimacy, when they almost caress each other by movements of the head; or when the free horses neigh to one another so that the woods echo, when they are gathered on the plains in a big herd as if at a public meeting—assume then that they really could make themselves understood to one another.

But then there was one horse that was all alone. Now when

this horse heard the call, when he saw that the herd was gathering in the evening, and he understood that they were about to hold a meeting, then he came running in the hope that he might learn something about life and its ways. He listened carefully to all that the elders had to say about how no horse should think himself fortunate until he is dead, how the horse of all creatures is the most subject to the tragic changes of fate. And now the elder went over the many agonies; to suffer hunger and cold, to all but kill oneself through overwork, to be kicked by a cruel driver, to be abused by unskilled persons whom not a single step you take will satisfy, yet who blame and punish the horse for their own blunders, and then at last some winter, when old age has come on, to be driven out into the bare woods.

At this point the meeting broke up and that horse who had come with such eagerness went away dejected: "by sorrow of the heart the spirit is broken" (Proverbs 15:13). He had understood perfectly all that had been said, but no one there had even as much as mentioned his sufferings. Yet each time he noticed the other horses hurrying off to a gathering he came running eagerly, hoping always now it would be spoken of. And each time he listened he went away with a heavy heart. He came to understand better and better what the others were concerned about, but he came to understand himself less and less, just because it seemed as though the others excluded him, although he, too, was present.

Purity of Heart, pp. 155-57 (*SV* XI 98-99)

The Confessor and the Penitent

What is the relationship of philosophy and history?

Philosophy relates to history as a confessor to the penitent, and like a confessor, it ought to have a supple and searching ear for the penitent's secrets; but after having listened to a full account of his confession, it must then be able to make this appear to the penitent as an "other." And as the penitent individual is able to rattle off the fateful events of his life chronologically, even recite them entertainingly, but cannot himself see through them, so history is able to proclaim with loud pathos the rich full life of the race, but must leave its explanation to the elder (philosophy). History can then experience the pleasant surprise that while at first it would almost disown its philosophic counterpart, it afterwards identifies itself with this conception of philosophy to such a degree that, finally, it would regard this as the essential truth, the other as mere appearance.

The Concept of Irony, p. 48 (*SV* I 70)

The Self-assured Policeman

What is the authority of the comic?

The more one suffers, the more, I believe, has one a sense for the comic. It is only by the deepest suffering that one acquires true authority in the use of the comic, an authority which by one word transforms as by magic the reasonable creature one calls man into a caricature. This authority is like the self-assurance of the policeman when he lays hand upon his stick without ceremony and permits no back-talk and no obstruction of the street. The man who is struck would retort, he makes a protest, he would be treated with respect as a citizen, he threatens an investigation; at that instant the next rap of the stick follows, with the warning, "Hold your tongue, keep moving, don't stand still."

Quidam in *Stages on Life's Way*, p. 231 (*SV* VIII 63-64)

The Darkroom Search

Is love blind?

They say that love makes blind, and by this they explain the phenomenon. In case a man going into a dark room to fetch something were to reply to my advice that he carry a light by saying, "The thing I am seeking is only a trifle, therefore I carry no light"—ah, then I could understand him perfectly. On the other hand, when the same man takes me aside and confides to me in a mysterious manner that the thing he went to fetch was of the utmost importance, and therefore he could do it blindly—ah, I wonder how my poor mortal head might be able to follow the high flight of this speech. Even if for fear of offending him I might refrain from laughter, as soon as his back was turned I could not help laughing. But at love nobody laughs.

The Young Man in *Stages on Life's Way*, p. 51 (*SV* VII 37)

The Test

How shall we sharpen the distinction between direct and indirect communication?

That indirect communication requires faith can be demonstrated very simply in the case of a purely human relationship, if only it be remembered that faith in the most eminent sense has to do with the God-Man.[21] Let us carry out the demonstration, and to this end let us take the relationship between two lovers. I assume first this relationship: the lover gives the beloved assurance of his love in the most burning expressions, and his whole nature corresponds to this assurance, is almost sheer adoration—then he asks the beloved, "*Do you believe that I love you?*" Then the beloved answers, "*Yes, I believe.*" This assuredly is the way we use the word. Now let us assume, on the other hand, that the lover gets a notion to wish to put the beloved to the test, whether she believes him. What does he do then? He cuts off all direct communication, he transforms himself into a duplex being; to all appearance it is as plausible to take him for a deceiver as for the faithful lover. Thus he makes himself a riddle. But what is a riddle? A riddle is a question. And what does the question ask? It asks whether she believes him.—I do not decide whether he has a right to do this, I am merely following the indications of thought; and in any case it should be remembered that the maieutic teacher does this very thing up to a certain point; he erects the dialectical duplexity, but with the opposite intent of turning the other person away from him, of turning him in upon himself, of making him free, not of drawing the man towards him.—One will easily see what is the difference in the lover's behavior in these two instances. In the first case he asks the question directly: "Do you believe me?" In the second case the question is the same, but he has made himself an interrogation. He may perhaps have cause to regret bitterly that he presumed to do such a thing—I am not concerned here with such possibilities, I am merely following the indications of thought. And from a dialectical point of view it is quite certain that the latter method is a far more fundamental way of eliciting faith. The aim of the latter method is to reveal the heart of the beloved in a choice; for in this duplex possibility she is obliged to choose which character she believes to be the true one.

Anti-Climacus in *Training in Christianity*, p. 141
(*SV* XVI 136-37)

The Anonymous Disciple

What does the true disciple do?

"One must go further, one must go further." This impulse to go further is an ancient thing in the world. Heraclitus the obscure, who deposited his thoughts in his writings and his writings in the Temple of Diana (for his thoughts had been his armor during his life, and therefore he hung them up in the temple of the goddess), Heraclitus the obscure said, "One cannot pass twice through the same stream." Heraclitus the obscure had a disciple who did not stop with that, he went further and added, "One cannot do it even once." Poor Heraclitus, to have such a disciple! By this amendment the thesis of Heraclitus was so improved that it became an Eleatic thesis which denies movement, and yet that disciple desired only to be a disciple of Heraclitus . . . . . and to go further—not back to the position Heraclitus had abandoned.[22]

Johannes de Silentio in *Fear and Trembling*, p. 132 (*SV* V 111)

33

The Author of the Proofs

*By what arguments or means do we come to understand
that "all things work together for good—
IF we love God"?*

Imagine a man equipped if possible in more than an extraordinary measure with intellectual gifts, with a profundity in pondering, a keenness in comprehending, a clarity in presentation, a thinker the like of whom was never seen and never shall be seen; he has pondered upon the nature of God, upon the fact that God is love, upon what follows from this as a consequence, that the world also must be the best, and all things must work together for good. And what he has fathomed he has elucidated in a book which is regarded as the possession of the whole race and the object of its pride; it is translated into all languages, referred to on all occasions of scientific discussion, and from this book the parsons fetch their proofs. This thinker has lived hitherto unacquainted with the world, protected by favorable conditions, which indeed are required for scientific research. Then it befalls him to come to grief in consequence of an important decision; he must act in a difficult situation and at a critical moment. And this action entails a consequence which he had not in the least anticipated, a consequence which plunges him and many others into misery. This is a consequence of his act—and yet he is convinced that he could not have acted otherwise than he did act after the most honest reflection. So here it is not a question of misfortune merely, but of blame which attaches to him, however blameless he knows himself to be. Now he is wounded; there awakens in his soul a doubt whether this also can work together for his good. And in him, the thinker, this doubt at once takes the direction of thought: whether after all God is

34

love—for in the believer doubt takes another direction, that of concern about himself. Over this man the objective concern acquires more and more power, so that at last he hardly knows where he his. In this situation he has recourse to a parson who is not personally acquainted with him. He opens his mind to him and seeks comfort. The clergyman, who is abreast of the times and is a thinker of sorts, would now prove to him that this also must be for the best and work for his good, since God is love; but he soon ascertains that he is not the man to maintain his side in a conflict of thought with this unknown individual. After several vain attempts, the clergyman says: "Well I have only one counsel left to give you; there is a book about the love of God by so and so, read it, study it, if that does not help you, no man can help you." The unknown man replies, "I myself am the author of this book."

Christian Discourses, pp. 206-07 (*SV* XIII 188-89)

The Swindler and the Widow's Mite

Is charitable intent essential to an act of charity or mercy?

Take the story about the woman who placed the two pennies in the temple-treasury, but let us poetize a little variation. The two pennies were for her a great sum, which she had not quickly accumulated. She had saved for a long time in order to get them saved up, and then she had hidden them wrapped in a little cloth in order to bring them when she herself went up to the temple. But a swindler had detected that she possessed this money, had tricked her out of it, and had exchanged the cloth for an identical piece which was utterly empty—something which the widow did not know. Thereupon she went up to the temple, placed, as she intended, the two pennies, that is, nothing, in the temple-treasury: I wonder if Christ would not still have said what he said of her, that "she gave more than all the rich?"

Works of Love, p. 294 (*SV* XII 304)

36

The Interrupted Wise Man

What is the relation of presumption and wisdom?

If someone talked with a wise man, and immediately upon the first words of the wise man, he interrupted him with his thanks, because he now needed no more help: what would this show other than that he did not talk with a wise man, but with a wise man whom he himself transformed into a fool?

Thoughts on Crucial Situations in Human Life, pp. 69-70
(*SV* VI 292)

The Speedy Arrest

*To what shall we compare the radical transparency
of conscience?*

A man seated in a glass case is not put to such embarrassment as is a man in his transparency before God. This is the factor of conscience. By the aid of conscience things are so arranged that the judicial report follows at once upon every fault, and that the guilty one himself must write it. But it is written with sympathetic ink and only becomes thoroughly clear when in eternity it is held up to the light, while eternity holds audit over the consciences. Substantially everyone arrives in eternity bringing with him and delivering the most accurate account of every least insignificance which he has committed or has left undone. Therefore to hold judgment in eternity is a thing

37

a child could manage; there is really nothing for a third person to do, everything, even to the most insignificant word is counted and in order. The case of the guilty man who journeys through life to eternity is like that of the murderer who with the speed of the railway train fled from the place where he perpetrated his crime. Alas, just under the railway coach where he sat ran the electric telegraph with its signal and the order for his apprehension at the next station. When he reached the station and alighted from the coach he was arrested. In a way he had himself brought the denunciation with him.

Anti-Climacus in *The Sickness unto Death*, p 255
(*SV* XV 173)

The Storm

Is knowledge changed when it is applied?

Let us imagine a pilot, and assume that he had passed every examination with distinction, but that he had not as yet been at sea. Imagine him in a storm; he knows everything he ought to do, but he has not known before how terror grips the seafarer when the stars are lost in the blackness of night; he has not known the sense of impotence that comes when the pilot sees the wheel in his hand become a plaything for the waves; he has not known how the blood rushes to the head when one tries to make calculations at such a moment; in short, he has had no conception of the change that takes place in the knower when he has to apply his knowledge.

Thoughts on Crucial Situations in Human Life, pp. 35-36
(*SV* VI 270)

The Two Artists

*What is the difference between requiring love of the
neighbor and finding lovableness
in the neighbor?*

. . . Suppose there were two artists, and the one said, "I have
travelled much and seen much in the world, but I have sought
in vain to find a man worth painting. I have found no face
with such perfection of beauty that I could make up my mind
to paint it. In every face I have seen one or another little fault.
Therefore I seek in vain." Would this indicate that this artist
was a great artist? On the other hand, the second one said,
"Well, I do not pretend to be a real artist; neither have I
travelled in foreign lands. But remaining in the little circle of
men who are closest to me, I have not found a face so insignificant or so full of faults that I still could not discern in it
a more beautiful side and discover something glorious. Therefore I am happy in the art I practice. It satisfies me without my
making any claim to being an artist." Would this not indicate
that precisely this one was the artist, one who by bringing a
certain something with him found then and there what the
much-travelled artist did not find anywhere in the world, perhaps because he did not bring a certain something with him!
Consequently the second of the two was the artist. Would it
not be sad, too, if what is intended to beautify life could only
be a curse upon it, so that *art*, instead of making life beautiful
for us, only fastidiously discovers that not one of us is beautiful. Would it not be sadder still, and still more confusing, if
love also should be only a curse because its demand could only
make it evident that none of us is worth loving, instead of
love's being recognized precisely by its loving enough to be
able to find some lovableness in all of us, consequently loving
enough to be able to love all of us.

Works of Love, pp. 156-57 (*SV* XII 153-54)

The King and the Maiden

To what shall we compare
the divine love that overcomes the infinite distance
between human sin and the holiness of God?

Suppose there was a king who loved a humble maiden.[23] But
the reader has perhaps already lost his patience, seeing that
our beginning sounds like a fairy tale, and is not in the least
systematic. So the very learned Polos found it tiresome that
Socrates always talked about meat and drink and doctors, and
similar unworthy trifles, which Polos deemed beneath him
(*Gorgias*).[24] But did not the Socratic manner of speech have
at least one advantage, in that he himself and all others were
from childhood equipped with the necessary prerequisites for
understanding it? And would it not be desirable if I could confine the terms of my argument to meat and drink, and did not
need to bring in kings, whose thoughts are not always like
those of other men, if they are indeed kingly. But perhaps I
may be pardoned the extravagance, seeing that I am only a
poet, proceeding now to unfold the carpet of my discourse
(recalling the beautiful saying of Themistocles),[25] lest its
workmanship be concealed by the compactness of its folding.

Suppose then a king who loved a humble maiden. The
heart of the king was not polluted by the wisdom that is loudly
enough proclaimed; he knew nothing of the difficulties that
the understanding discovers in order to ensnare the heart,
which keep the poets so busy, and make their magic formulas
necessary. It was easy to realize his purpose. Every statesman
feared his wrath and dared not breathe a word of displeasure;
every foreign state trembled before his power, and dared not
omit sending ambassadors with congratulations for the nup-
tials; no courtier grovelling in the dust dared wound him, lest
his own head be crushed. Then let the harp be tuned, let the
songs of the poets begin to sound, and let all be festive while
love celebrates its triumph. For love is exultant when it unites

equals, but it is triumphant when it makes that which was unequal equal in love.[26]—Then there awoke in the heart of the king an anxious thought; who but a king who thinks kingly thoughts would have dreamed of it! He spoke to no one about his anxiety; for if he had, each courtier would doubtless have said: "Your majesty is about to confer a favor upon the maiden, for which she can never be sufficiently grateful her whole life long." This speech would have moved the king to wrath, so that he would have commanded the execution of the courtier for high treason against the beloved, and thus he would in still another way have found his grief increased. So he wrestled with his troubled thoughts alone. Would she be happy in the life at his side? Would she be able to summon confidence enough never to remember what the king wished only to forget, that he was king and she had been a humble maiden? For if this memory were to waken in her soul, and like a favored lover sometimes steal her thoughts away from the king, luring her reflections into the seclusion of a secret grief; or if this memory sometimes passed through her soul like the shadow of death over the grave: where would then be the glory of their love? Then she would have been happier had she remained in her obscurity, loved by an equal, content in her humble cottage; but confident in her love, and cheerful early and late. What a rich abundance of grief is here laid bare, like ripened grain bent under the weight of its fruitfulness, merely awaiting the time of the harvest, when the thought of the king will thresh out all its seed of sorrow! For even if the maiden would be content to become as nothing, this could not satisfy the king, precisely because he loved her, and because it was harder for him to be her benefactor than to lose her. And suppose she could not even understand him? For while we are thus speaking foolishly of human relationships, we may suppose a difference of mind between them such as to render an understanding impossible. What a depth of grief slumbers not in this unhappy love, who dares to rouse it! . . .

Moved by love, the God[27] is thus eternally resolved to reveal himself. But as love is the motive so love must also be the end; for it would be a contradiction for the God to have a motive and an end which did not correspond. His love is a love of the learner, and his aim is to win him. For it is only in love that the unequal can be made equal, and it is only in equality or unity that an understanding can be effected. . . .

But this love is through and through unhappy, for how great is the difference between them! It may seem a small matter for the God to make himself understood, but this is not so easy of accomplishment if he is to refrain from annihilating the unlikeness that exists between them.

Let us not jump too quickly to a conclusion at this point. . . . Much is heard in the world about unhappy love, and we all know what this means: the lovers are prevented from realizing their union, the causes being many and various. There exists another kind of unhappy love, the theme of our present discourse, for which there is no perfect earthly parallel, though by dint of speaking foolishly a little while we may make shift to conceive it through an earthly figure. The unhappiness of this love does not come from the inability of the lovers to realize their union, but from their inability to understand one another. This grief is infinitely more profound than that of which men commonly speak, since it strikes at the very heart of love, and wounds for an eternity; not like that other misfortune which touches only the temporal and the external, and which for the magnanimous is as a sort of jest over the inability of the lovers to realize their union here in time. This infinitely deeper grief is essentially the prerogative of the superior, since only he likewise understands the misunderstanding. . . .

Our problem is now before us, and we invite the poet, unless he is already engaged elsewhere, or belongs to the number of those who must be driven out from the house of mourning, together with the flute-players and the other noise-makers, before gladness can enter in.[28] The poet's task will be to find a solution, some point of union, where love's understanding may be realized in truth, the God's anxiety be set at rest, his sorrow banished. For the divine love is that unfathomable love which cannot rest content with that which the beloved might in his folly prize as happiness.

A

The union might be brought about by an elevation of the learner. The God would then take him up unto himself, transfigure him, fill his cup with millennial joys (for a thousand years are as one day in his sight), and let the learner forget the misunderstanding in tumultuous joy. Alas, the learner might perhaps be greatly inclined to prize such happiness as this. How wonderful suddenly to find his fortune made, like the humble maiden, because the eye of the God happened to rest upon him! And how wonderful also to be his helper in taking all this in vain, deceived by his own heart! Even the noble king could perceive the difficulty of such a method, for he was not without insight into the human heart, and understood that the maiden was at bottom deceived; and no one is so terribly deceived as he who does not himself suspect it, but is as if enchanted by a change in the outward habiliments of his existence.

The union might be brought about by the God's showing himself to the learner and receiving his worship, causing him to forget himself over the divine apparition. Thus the king might have shown himself to the humble maiden in all the pomp of his power, causing the sun of his presence to rise over her cottage, shedding a glory over the scene, and making her forget herself in worshipful admiration. Alas, and this might have satisfied the maiden, but it could not satisfy the king, who desired not his own glorification but hers. It was this that made his grief so hard to bear, his grief that she could not understand him; but it would have been still harder for him to deceive her. And merely to give his love for her an imperfect expression was in his eyes a deception, even though no one understood him and reproaches sought to mortify his soul.

Not in this manner then can their love be made happy, except perhaps in appearance, namely the learner's and the

43

maiden's, but not the Teacher's and the king's, whom no delusion can satisfy. . . .

B

The union must therefore be brought about in some other way. Let us here again recall Socrates, for what was the Socratic ignorance if not an expression for his love of the learner, and for his sense of equality with him? . . . In the Socratic conception the teacher's love would be merely that of a deceiver if he permitted the disciple to rest in the belief that he really owed him anything, instead of fulfilling the function of the teacher to help the learner become sufficient to himself. But when the God becomes a Teacher, his love cannot be merely seconding and assisting, but is creative, giving a new being to the learner, or as we have called him, the man born anew; by which designation we signify the transition from nonbeing to being. The truth then is that the learner owes the Teacher everything. But this is what makes it so difficult to effect an understanding: that the learner becomes as nothing and yet is not destroyed; that he comes to owe everything to the Teacher and yet retains his confidence. . . .

Since we found that the union could not be brought about by an elevation it must be attempted by a descent. Let the learner be x. In this x we must include the lowliest; for if even Socrates refused to establish a false fellowship with the clever, how can we suppose that the God would make a distinction! In order that the union may be brought about, the God must therefore become the equal of such an one, and so he will appear in the likeness of the humblest. But the humblest is one who must serve others, and the God will therefore appear in the form of a *servant*. But this servant-form is no mere outer garment, like the king's beggar-cloak, which therefore flutters loosely about him and betrays the king;[29] it is not like the filmy summer-cloak of Socrates, which though woven of nothing yet both conceals and reveals.[30] It is his true form and figure. For this is the unfathomable nature of love, that it desires equality with the beloved,

44

not in jest merely, but in earnest and truth. And it is the omnipotence of the love which is so resolved that it is able to accomplish its purpose, which neither Socrates nor the king could do, whence their assumed figures constituted after all a kind of deceit. . . .

But the servant-form was no mere outer garment, and therefore the God must suffer all things, endure all things, make experience of all things. He must suffer hunger in the desert, he must thirst in the time of his agony, he must be forsaken in death,[31] absolutely like the humblest—behold the man! . . .[32]

Every other form of revelation would be a deception in the eyes of love; for either the learner would first have to be changed, and the fact concealed from him that this was necessary (but love does not alter the beloved, it alters itself); or there would be permitted to prevail a frivolous ignorance of the fact that the entire relationship was a delusion. . . .

Now if someone were to say: "This poem of yours is the most wretched piece of plagiarism ever perpetrated, for it is neither more nor less than what every child knows," I suppose I must blush with shame to hear myself called a liar. But why the most wretched? Every poet who steals, steals from some other poet, and in so far as we are all equally wretched; indeed, my own theft is perhaps less harmful since it is more readily discovered.

Johannes Climacus in *Philosophical Fragments*, pp. 31-43
(*SV* VI 28-36)

The Freeze of the Mime

What is the relation of eternity and the moment?

Paul says that the world will pass away "in an instant in the twinkling of an eye" (ἐν ἀτόμῳ καὶ ἐν ῥιπῇ ὀφθαλμοῦ). By that he also expresses the thought that the instant is commensurable with eternity, because the instant of destruction expresses at the same instant eternity. Allow me to illustrate what I mean, and forgive me if there is found anything offensive in the parable I employ. Here in Copenhagen there once upon a time were two actors, who perhaps hardly reflected that a deeper significance might be found in their performance. They came on the stage, placed themselves opposite one another, and then began a pantomime representation of some passionate conflict. When the pantomimic play was in full swing, and the spectators were following the play with keen expectancy of what was to come after, the actors suddenly came to a stop and remained motionless, as though they were petrified in the pantomimic expression of the instant. This may produce a most comical effect, because the instant becomes accidentally commensurable with the eternal. The effect of sculpture is due to the fact that the eternal expression is expressed eternally; the comic effect, on the other hand, by the fact that the accidental expression was eternalized.

Vigilius Haufniensis in *The Concept of Dread*, p. 79n
(*SV* VI 176n)

The Costume of the Actor

What does it mean to love one's neighbor?

To love one's neighbor means, while remaining within the earthly distinctions allotted to one, essentially to will to exist equally for every human being without exception. . . .

Consider for a moment the world which lies before you in all its variegated multiplicity; it is like looking at a play, only the plot is vastly more complicated. Every individual in this innumerable throng is by his differences a particular something; he exhibits a definiteness but essentially he is something other than this—but this we do not get to see here in life. Here we see only what role the individual plays and how he does it. It is like a play. But when the curtain falls, the one

47

who played the king, and the one who played the beggar, and all the others—they are all quite alike, all one and the same: actors. And when in death the curtain falls on the stage of actuality (for it is a confused use of language if one speaks about the curtain being rolled up on the stage of the eternal at the time of death, because the eternal is no stage—it is truth), then they also are all one; they are human beings. All are that which they essentially were, something we did not see because of the difference we see; they are human beings. The stage of art is like an enchanted world. But just suppose that some evening a common absent-mindedness confused all the actors so they thought they really were what they were representing. Would this not be, in contrast to the enchantment of art, what one might call the enchantment of an evil spirit, a bewitchment? And likewise suppose that in the enchantment of actuality (for we are, indeed, all enchanted, each one bewitched by his own distinctions) our fundamental ideas became confused so that we thought ourselves essentially to be the roles we play. Alas, but is this not the case? It seems to be forgotten that the distinctions of earthly existence are only like an actor's costume or like a travelling cloak and that every individual should watchfully and carefully keep the fastening cords of this outer garment loosely tied, never in obstinate knots, so that in the moment of transformation the garment can easily be cast off, and yet we all have enough knowledge of art to be offended if an actor, when he is supposed to cast off his disguise in the moment of transformation, runs out on the stage before getting the cords loose. But, alas, in actual life one laces the outer garment of distinction so tightly that it completely conceals the external character of this garment of distinction, and the inner glory of equality never, or very rarely, shines through, something it should do and ought to do constantly.

Works of Love, pp. 92-96 (*SV* XLL 86-91)

48

The Three-Cent Beer

Can numbers reveal the vitality of religious existence?

They tell a ludicrous story about an innkeeper, a story moreover which is related incidentally by one of my pseudonyms,[33]
but I would use it again because it has always seemed to me to
have a profound meaning. It is said that he sold his beer by
the bottle for a cent less than he paid for it; and when a certain man said to him, "How does that balance the account?
That means to spend money," he replied, "No, my friend, it's
the big number that does it"—big number, that also in our
time is the almighty power. When one has laughed at this
story, one would do well to take to heart the lesson which warns
against the power which number exercises over the imagination. For there can be no doubt that this innkeeper knew very
well that one bottle of beer which he sold for 3 cents meant a
loss of 1 cent when it cost him 4 cents. Also with regard to
ten bottles the innkeeper will be able to hold fast that it is a
loss. But 100,000 bottles! Here the big number stirs the imagination, the round number runs away with it, and the innkeeper becomes dazed—it's a profit, says he, for the big number does it. So also with the calculation which arrives at a
Christian nation by adding up units which are not Christian,
getting the result by means of the notion that the big number
does it.

Attack Upon "Christendom," pp. 30-31 (*SV* XIX 40-41)

Bang, the Earth is Round

Why can't one prove himself to be sanely in possession of his faculties if he tells the truth objectively?

A patient in . . . an institution seeks to escape, and actually succeeds in effecting his purpose by leaping out of a window, and prepares to start on the road to freedom, when the thought strikes him (shall I say sanely enough or madly enough?): "When you come to town you will be recognized, and you will at once be brought back here again; hence you need to prepare yourself fully to convince everyone by the objective truth of what you say, that all is in order as far as your sanity is concerned." As he walks along and thinks about this, he sees a ball lying on the ground, picks it up, and puts it into the tail pocket of his coat. Every step he takes the ball strikes him, politely speaking, on his hinder parts, and every time it thus strikes him he says: "Bang, the earth is round." He comes to the city, and at once calls on one of his friends; he wants to convince him that he is not crazy, and therefore walks back and forth, saying continually: "Bang, the earth is round!" But is not the earth round? Does the asylum still crave yet another sacrifice for this opinion, as in the time when all men believed it to be flat as a pancake? Or is a man who hopes to prove that he is sane, by uttering a generally accepted and generally respected objective truth, insane? And yet it was clear to the physician that the patient was not yet cured; though it is not to be thought that the cure would consist in getting him to accept the opinion that the earth is flat.[34]

Johannes Climacus in *Concluding Unscientific Postscript*
p. 174 (*SV* IX 162-63)

50

The Foolish Day-Laborer

Why does the invitation to faith appear to be absurd?

If I were to imagine to myself a day-laborer and the mightiest emperor that ever lived, and were to imagine that this mighty Emperor took a notion to send for the poor man, who never dreamed, "neither had it entered into his heart to believe,"[35] that the Emperor knew of his existence, and who therefore would think himself indescribably fortunate if merely he was permitted once to see the Emperor, and would recount it to his children and children's children as the most important event of his life—but suppose the Emperor sent for him and informed him that he wished to have him for his son-in-law . . . . . what then? Then the laborer, humanly, would become somewhat or very much puzzled, shame-faced, and embarrassed, and it would seem to him, quite humanly (and this is the human element in it), something exceedingly strange, something quite mad, the last thing in the world about which he would say a word to anybody else, since he himself in his own mind was not far from explaining it by supposing (as his neighbors would be busily doing as soon as possible) that the Emperor wanted to make a fool of him, so that the poor man would be the laughing-stock of the whole town, his picture in the papers, the story of his espousal to the Emperor's daughter the theme of ballad-mongers. This thing, however, of becoming the Emperor's son-in-law might readily be subjected to the tests of reality, so that the laborer would be able to ascertain how far the Emperor was serious in this matter, or whether he merely wanted to make fun of the poor fellow, render him unhappy for the rest of his life, and help him to find his way to the mad-house, for the *quid nimis*[36] is in evidence, which with such infinite ease can turn into its opposite.

51

A small expression of favor the laborer would be able to get through his head; it would be understood in the market-town by "the highly respected cultured public," by all ballad-mongers, in short, by the 5 times 100,000 persons who dwelt in that market-town, which with respect to its population was even a very big city, but with respect to possessing under-standing of and sense for the extraordinary was a very small market-town—but this thing of becoming the Emperor's son-in-law was far too much. And suppose now that this was not an external reality but an inward thing, so that factual proofs could not help the laborer to certitude but faith itself was the facticity, and so it was all left to faith whether he possessed humble courage enough to dare to believe it (for impudent courage cannot help one to *believe*)—how many laboring men were there likely to be who possessed this courage? But he who had not this courage would be offended; the extraordi-nary would seem to him almost like mockery of him. He would then perhaps honestly and plainly admit, "Such a thing is too high for me, I cannot get it into my head; it seems to me, if I may blurt it straight out, foolishness."

Anti-Climacus in *The Sickness unto Death*,
pp. 215-16 (*SV* XV 137-38)

The Untouched Food

*What is the difference between faith and the
profession of faith?*

If there was a certain kind of food, an article of food which, for one reason or another, had such significance for a man that it was completely tied up with his most intimate feelings (we may imagine a national dish, or a food which has religious significance), and as a result of this it was impossible for him to remain silent if this food was scoffed at or even referred to disparagingly: then it would be natural that, if this happened in his presence, he would admit and confess his own emotions. But let us imagine the relationship somewhat altered. We imagine this man gathered in company with several others, and this food is set before them. When it is offered them, each of the guests says personally: "This is the most excellent and precious of all foods." Certainly, if that man of whom we are speaking discovers with astonishment, or believes that he discovers, that the guests do not eat of this dish, that they leave it untouched, that they confine themselves to other foods, while they still say that that food is the most excellent and precious: is the man in that case required to acknowledge his own conviction? There is no one indeed who contradicts him, no one who says anything other than what he says.

The Gospel of Suffering, pp. 141-42 (*SV* XI 297)

The Candidate Seeking

How does civil religion stand in relation to the absolute?

Imagine a candidate in theology. Let it be me, I also indeed am a candidate in theology. He has already been a candidate for some few years, and now he enters upon that period of life when it is said of him that "he is seeking." "A candidate in theology"—"seeks": when the riddle is proposed in these terms, one does not need a particularly lively imagination to guess at once what it is he "seeks"—of course it is the kingdom of God (Matt. 6:33). However, your guess is wrong; no, he seeks something else, a parish, a living—he seeks this almost absolutely; in other respects the affair has nothing to do with the absolute, nor does it betray any impression of the absolute.

He seeks. In his search he runs from Herod to Pilate, recommends himself before ministers and secretaries, he writes and writes, one sheet of stamped paper after another—for the supplication must be written on paper which bears the stamp of the government, perhaps one might call this the impression of the absolute, otherwise there is nothing of the sort here. A year passes; he had almost worn himself out with his running and seeking, which can hardly be said to be in the service of the absolute, except (as has been remarked) that he seeks "absolutely everything." Finally he gets what he sought; he finds the Scriptural text confirmed, "Seek and ye shall find"; but the absolute he did not find, it was only a small living—but after all it was not the absolute he was seeking. Still, he is at peace; and indeed he is now in need of repose, so that he can rest himself and his legs after the much seeking. However, when he makes himself more precisely acquainted with the income of the living, he discovers to his dismay that it is a few hundred dollars less than he had supposed. This is exceedingly calamitous for him, as, humanly speaking, one can well understand and can agree with him about it. It is doubly unpleasant for him because at the same time he has found something else which he sought concurrently, namely, a wife, which quite obviously is related to a living, and maybe each year more so. He loses heart. He buys again a sheet of stamped paper, is already afoot to put in a supplication to be allowed to withdraw. However, some of his friends get him to give this up. So the thing is decided. He becomes a parson. Now he is to be installed by the Dean and is himself to deliver the inaugural address. The Dean is a man of intelligence and learning, not without an eye for world-history, much to his own profit and that of the congregation. He presents the new parson to the congregation, makes an address, and chooses for his text the words of the Apostle, "Lo, we have left all and followed Thee." Upon this text he speaks pithily and forcefully; he shows that, especially in view of the movements of these times, the minister of the Word must now be prepared to sacrifice everything, though it were life and blood—and the very rever-

54

end speaker knows that the young man he installs (yes, as I have said, we can very well understand the young man, for that is human; but we cannot so well understand the Dean) happened to be desirous of withdrawing because the living was a few hundred dollars too little. Thereupon the new parson mounts the pulpit. And the Gospel for the day, upon which he is to preach, is—very opportunely!—"Seek ye first the kingdom of God." Truly, when one recalls what this young man had to go through with during the laborious year of seeking, this "seek first" is the last thing one would be likely to think of! So he preaches. And it was in every respect a good sermon; even the Bishop, who was present, said "It was a capital sermon, and excellently delivered, he is really an orator."—"Yes, but then, if it were to be judged Christianly."—"Good gracious, it was an entirely Christian sermon, it was the sound, unalloyed doctrine, and the stress he laid upon *first* to seek God's kingdom was not without thrilling effect."—"Yes, but now, Christianly judged, I mean, how far was there here a correspondence between the preacher's life and his discourse? I could hardly free myself entirely from the thought that the speaker—who for me is a true picture of us all—cannot precisely be said with truth to have sought first God's kingdom."—"That's not at all required."—"Oh, excuse me, but that is what he preached about, that we first should seek God's kingdom." "Quite so, that is exactly the way he should preach, that is what is required of him. It is the doctrine that has to be attended to, the doctrine has to be preached pure and unalloyed."

This represents about the way Christendom stands related to Christianity, the absolute.

Judge for Yourselves!, pp. 126-28 (*SV* XVII 143-45)

The Illegible Letter

*To what shall we compare the pathos
of grieving loneliness?*

If a man possessed a letter which he knew, or believed, contained information bearing upon what he must regard as his life's happiness, but the writing was pale and fine, almost illegible—then would he read it with restless anxiety and with all possible passion, in one moment getting one meaning, in the next another, depending on his belief that, having made out one word with certainty he could interpret the rest thereby; but he would never arrive at anything except the same uncertainty with which he began. He would stare more and more anxiously, but the more he stared, the less he would see. His eyes would sometimes fill with tears; but the oftener this happened the less he would see. In the course of time, the writing would become fainter and more illegible, until at last the paper itself would crumble away, and nothing would be left to him except the tears in his eyes.

"A" in *Either/Or*, I, p. 188 (*SV* II 176)

A Visit to the Doctor

Can medicine abolish the anxious conscience?

In our time (this is truth, and it is significant for the Christianity of our time), in our time it is the physician who exercises the cure of souls. People have perhaps an unfounded dread of calling in the parson, who, however, in our time would talk possibly pretty much like the physician. So they call in the physician. And he knows what to do: [Dr.]: "You must travel to a watering-place, and then must keep a riding-horse, for it is possible to ride away from bees in the bonnet, and then diversion, diversion, plenty of diversion, you must ensure yourself of having every evening a cheerful game of poker, on the other hand you should not eat much in the evening directly before going to bed, and finally see that the bedroom is well aired—this will surely help."—[Patient]: "To relieve an anxious conscience?"—[Dr.]: "Bosh! Get out with that stuff! An anxious conscience! No such thing exists any more, it is a reminiscence of the childhood of the race. There is no enlightened and cultivated parson who would think of coming out with such a thing—I mean to say, outside the Sunday service, which is a different matter. No, let us never begin here with an anxious conscience, for thus we might soon turn the whole house into a madhouse. I am so minded that if I had in my employ a servant, however excellent in other respects, whom I should be loath to lose and should greatly miss—if I observed that he or she was meddling with the experience of an anxious conscience, I would give unconditional notice to quit my service. That would be the last thing I would tolerate in my house. If it were my own child, he would have to seek other quarters."—[Patient]: "But, Doctor, this is an awfully anxious dread you have of a thing which you say does not exist, 'an anxious conscience'; one might almost think that it is a revenge upon you for wanting to do away with anguish of conscience—this anxious dread of yours is indeed like a revenge!"

Judge for Yourselves!, p. 210 (*SV* XVII 221)

The Water Spout

To what shall we compare our miscalculations about divine providence?

"A man should never lose his courage; when misfortunes tower most fearfully about him, there appears in the sky a helping hand." Thus spoke the Reverend Jesper Morten last evensong. Now I am in the habit of travelling much under the open sky, but I had never seen anything of the kind. A few days ago, however, while on a walking tour, some such phenomenon took place. It was not exactly a hand, but something like an arm which stretched out of the sky. I began to ponder: it occurred to me that if only Jesper Morten were here, he might be able to decide whether this was the phenomenon he referred to. As I stood there in the midst of my thoughts, I was addressed by a wayfarer. Pointing up to the sky, he said: "Do you see that waterspout? They are very rare in these parts; sometimes they carry whole houses away with them." "The Lord preserve us," thought I, "is that a waterspout?" and took to my heels as fast as I could. I wonder what the Reverend Jesper Morten would have done in my place?

"A" in *Either/Or*, I, pp. 26-27 (*SV* II 30)

The Rigorous Coachman

Of what is the human spirit capable?

Once upon a time there was a rich man who ordered from abroad at a high price a pair of entirely faultless and high-bred horses which he desired to have for his own pleasure and for the pleasure of driving them himself. Then about a year or two elapsed. Anyone who previously had known these horses would not have been able to recognize them again. Their eyes had become dull and drowsy, their gait lacked style and decision, they couldn't endure anything, they couldn't hold out, they hardly could be driven four miles without having to stop on the way, sometimes they came to a standstill as he sat for all he was worth attempting to drive them, besides they had acquired all sorts of vices and bad habits, and in spite of the fact that they of course got fodder in overabundance, they were falling off in flesh day by day. Then he had the King's coachman called. He drove them for a month—in the whole region there was not a pair of horses that held their heads so proudly, whose glance was so fiery, whose gait was so handsome, no other pair of horses that could hold out so long, though it were to trot for more than a score of miles at a stretch without stopping. How came this about? It is easy to see. The owner, who without being a coachman pretended to be such, drove them in accordance with the horses' understanding of what it is to drive; the royal coachman drove them in accordance with the coachman's understanding of what it is to drive.

So it is with us men. Oh, when I think of myself and of the countless men I have learnt to know, I have often said to myself despondently, "Here are talents and powers and capacities enough—but the coachman is lacking." Through a long period of time, we men, from generation to generation, have been, if

59

I may so say, driven (to stick to the figure) in accordance with the horses' understanding of what it is to drive, we are directed, brought up, educated in accordance with man's conception of what it is to be a man. Behold therefore what we lack: exaltation, and what follows in turn from this, that we only can stand so little, impatiently employ at once the means of the instant, and in our impatience desire instantly to see the reward of our labour, which just for this reason is deferred.

Once it was different. Once there was a time when it pleased the Deity (if I may venture to say so) to be Himself the coachman; and He drove the horses in accordance with the coachman's understanding of what it is to drive. Oh, what was a man not capable of at that time!

For Self-Examination, pp. 104-05 (*SV* XVII 121-22)

Periander

Can wisdom survive amid the hazards of power?

Periander was a son of Kypselus of the Heraclidian race, and he succeeded his father as tyrant of Corinth. It is said of him that he always talked like a wise man and constantly acted like a maniac. It is very strange, and a continuation, as it were, of the madness of Periander, that he who characterized him by this clever saying did not himself know how significant it was. The rather shallow author[37] who vouches for it introduces in his simplicity the wise observation in the following way: "It is very extraordinary that the Greeks could have reckoned among the wise men such a fool as Periander." But a fool (*un fat*—such is the moralizing author's term) Periander was not. It would have been different if he had said that there was another Periander, Periander of Ambracia, with whom possibly

60

he was confused, or that there were only five wise men, or that historians had rather discordant notions, etc. So the gods understood the saying about Periander better, for in their wrath they so led him through life that they brought down the wise words as a mockery upon the head of the tyrant, who by his deeds brought his own words to shame.

When he became tyrant he distinguished himself by leniency, by justice towards the lowly, by wisdom among people of understanding. He kept his word and gave to the gods the statue he had promised, but it was paid for by women's jewels. Bold were his undertakings, and this was his saying: "Diligence accomplishes all things."

But beneath the leniency smoldered the fire of passion, and the word of wisdom concealed, until the moment arrived, the madness of his actions; and the bold undertakings gave proof of powers which remained the same in the transformed man. For Periander was transformed. He did not become another man, but he became two men, who could not be contained in the one man. These two were the wise man and the tyrant. That is to say, he became a monster. The occasion of his transformation is variously related. But this is certain, that it was only an occasion, for otherwise we cannot understand how he could be so changed. However, it is related that he had lived in criminal relations with his mother Gratia[38]—surely before he had yet heard his own fine saying: "Do not that which you have to keep secret."

And this is a saying of Periander's: "It is better to be feared than to be lamented."[39] He acted in accordance with this saying. He was the first who maintained a bodyguard and altered the government as the tyranny required, and ruled as tyrant over bondsmen, himself bound by the power he could not get rid of; for he himself said: "It is just as dangerous for a tyrant to lay down his command as to be deprived of it." He also got out of this difficulty by a clever device which subsequently will be described, and not even death subjected him to revenge—his name was inscribed upon an empty tomb. That this must be, Periander understood better than anyone, for he said: "Ill gain is father of a bad bargain."⁴⁰ "A tyrant," said he, "must have good will as a bodyguard, and not armed soldiers." Therefore the tyrant Periander was never secure, and the only refuge he found safe enough in death was an empty tomb in which he did not lie. This thought would have been expressed in a way evident to all if upon the empty tomb had been put the following inscription: Here RESTS a tyrant. The Greeks, however, did not do this. More placable, they permitted him in death to find peace in the motherly bosom of his native earth, and wrote upon the empty grave words which sound more beautiful in verse, but mean substantially this: Here Corinth, his native land, holds hidden in its bosom Periander the rich and wise. But this is untrue inasmuch as he does not lie there. A Greek writer composed another inscription, intended rather for the beholder, that the inscription might remind him "not to grieve because one never attains one's wish, but to accept with joy the dispensation of the gods, reflecting that the spirit of the wise Periander was quenched in despondency because he was unable to accomplish what he would."

This must suffice concerning his end, which teaches posterity about the wrath of the gods what Periander did not learn from it. The narrative recurs again to the occasion which led to the madness of Periander, which from that moment increased year by year to such a degree that he might have applied truly to himself a saying which, so it is said, a desperate man thousands of years later placed upon his escutcheon: "The more lost, the less repentant."⁴¹

As for the occasion, we will not attempt to decide whether it was that a rumor circulated about his criminal relations with his mother, so that he was mortified that people knew he "had done what one dared not mention"; or whether the occasion was an enigmatic response from his friend Thrasybolos, tyrant of Miletus, who indicated by sign language which, though not understood by the messenger (like the message of Tarquinius to his son) was well understood by Periander as a hint for the guidance of a tyrant; or finally whether the occasion was despair at having killed with a kick his beloved wife Lyside to whom he had given the name of Melissa. This we cannot decide. Everyone of these occurrences by itself would be sufficient: the ignominy of dishonor for the proud prince; the temptation of the significant enigma for the ambitious man; the torture of guilt for the unhappy lover. In union they would little by little have the effect that wickedness altered the understanding of the wise man, and exasperation deluded the soul of the ruler.

But when Periander was altered his fortune changed too. The proud saying, that it was better to be feared than to be lamented, fell upon his own head, upon his life of despair, and fell upon him in death. For he was lamented. It was lamentable even that he had uttered such a word, lamentable that the gods, who are the stronger, worked against him, whereas the deeper he sank in perdition, the less he understood in penitence their anger.

Melissa was a daughter of Prokles, tyrant in Epidauros. When the mother was slain, her two sons, Kypselos and Lykophron, the one seventeen years old and the other eighteen, fled to their maternal grandfather in Epidauros. There they remained some time, and when they returned to Corinth Prokles took leave of them by saying, "Do you know, children, who it is that killed your mother?" Upon Kypselos this saying made no impression, but Lykophron became silent. On returning to the paternal house he never deigned to reply to his father. At that Periander became exasperated and drove him away—and then learned (when by many questions he succeeded in prodding the memory of Kypselos) what it was Lykophron concealed under his silence. His wrath now pursued the outcast, and he commanded that no one might espouse the cause of the persecuted fugitive, who went from house to house until finally some friends took him in. Then Periander had it proclaimed that whoever offered hospitality to Lykophron or even spoke to him should die. Now no one dared to have anything to do with him, so that he must perish of hunger and wretchedness. Periander himself was moved and went to him when for four days and nights he had had neither meat nor drink. He invited him to be ruler in Corinth and lord of all his treasures, since he had now learned well what it is to defy his father. But Lykophron answered nothing. Finally he said, "You yourself are deserving of death, for you have transgressed your own commandment and spoken to me." Exasperated by this, Periander banished him to Corcyra, and his wrath was turned against Prokles, whom he vanquished, took captive and deprived of Epidauros.

Periander had now become an old man. Weary of power, he sought to lay it down. But, as he had said, "It is just as dangerous to lay down a tyranny as to be deprived of it," and from the tyrant one learns that it is also difficult to get rid of it. Kypselos was unfitted to rule, upon him not even the saying of Prokles had made an impression. So Lykophron was to succeed to the power. Periander sent a messenger to him, but to no effect. Finally he sent his daughter, that the obedient might persuade the disobedient and by her mild temper lead the erring one back to reverence for his father. But he remained in Corcyra. Then finally they decided to treat with one another, not as a father and son treat with one another in love, but like mortal enemies. They decided to exchange residences. Periander was to dwell in Corcyra and Lykophron was to be ruler in Corinth. Periander was about to start upon the journey, but the people of Corcyra had such a horror of him, and understood so well the intolerant spirit of the father and the son that they resolved to murder Lykophron, for they hoped that then Periander would not come. They did so, but by this they were not saved from Periander, who ordered three hundred of their children to be carried away and violated. But the gods prevented this, and Periander took it so to heart that he was unable to avenge his son that he resolved to put an end to himself. He summoned two young men and showed them a secret passage. Thereupon he commanded them to meet there the following day and slay the first man they encountered, burying him immediately. When these had gone he had five others summoned and gave the same order, namely that they were to wait at the passage and when they saw two young men they were to murder them and bury them at once. Then he had twice that number summoned and ordered them in the same way to slay the five whom they would meet and bury them on the spot where they were cut down. Then came Periander himself at the hour appointed and was murdered.[42]

Quidam in *Stages on Life's Way*, pp. 298-302 (*SV* VIII 133-36)

The Wise Men of Gotham

*Should "Christian philosophy" set out by subjecting
the adjective "Christian" to speculative
treatment?*

... It is quite in order to speculate within a presupposition, as
would seem to be the program of ... Christian philosophy in
adopting the qualifying predicate Christian. But if this philosophy which thus begins within a presupposition finally reaches
the point where it subjects its own presupposition to speculative treatment, and so speculates the presupposition away, what
then? Why then the presupposition was a mere fiction, a piece
of shadow-boxing. There is a story about the wise men of
Gotham, that they once saw a tree leaning out over the water
and thinking that the tree was thirsty were moved by sympathy to come to its assistance. To that end one of them took
hold of the tree, another clung to the first man's legs, and so on
until they formed a chain, all animated by the common idea
of helping the tree—under the presupposition that the first
man held fast. But what happens? The first man suddenly lets
go in order to spit on his hand so that he can take a better
hold—and what then? Why then the Gothamites fell into the
water, because the presupposition was given up.

Johannes Climacus in *Concluding Unscientific Postscript*,
p. 337 (*SV* X 74)

66

The Button

Should ethical actions always proceed "on principle"?

If a man had a little button sewn on the inner pocket of his coat "on principle" his otherwise unimportant and quite serviceable action would become charged with importance—it is not improbable that it would result in the formation of a society. . . . . "On principle" a man may interest himself in the founding of a brothel (there are plenty of social studies on the subject written by the health authorities), and the same man can "on principle" assist in the publication of a new Hymn Book because it is supposed to be the great need of the times. But it would be as unjustifiable to conclude from the first fact that he was debauched as it would, perhaps, be to conclude from the second that he read or sang hymns.

The Present Age, p. 74 (*SV* XIV 92)

The Perpetual Student

Can civil religion ever become authentically Christian?

In my youth there was a young man who never succeeded in passing his first examination in the university, but said regularly, "Next time I make it," for which cause we never called him by his proper name but by "Next time I make it." . . . However, now the time for protestations is past. . . . The reserve for protestations, the specie which a bank in order to be a bank always must possess, and which in this case Christianity's bank did possess—it has been consumed, ladies and gentlemen! Instead of being able to draw on the bank, a new bank must first be founded, by means of what in this case is the specie, namely, actions, actions in the role of a Christian.

Judge for Yourselves!, p. 150 (*SV* XVII 165-66)

The Embarrassed Leave-taking

*To what shall we compare an author who cannot
ever arrive at a conclusion?*

When a clergyman has luckily reached the third point of his
sermon and already is so far along in it that one who knows
the proportions of clerical elocution ventures with a good deal
of security to assume that he is about to hum and say Amen—
then it may be anguishing when he, instead of pronouncing the
significant Amen, becomes gossipy and adds one period after
another, while the knowing hearer may say that essentially the
sermon is over and essentially the Amen has been said. This
is an example of fortuitous length, recognizable by the fact
that it begins where, essentially viewed, the Amen should
have been said. One knows instances of people who, embarrassed and embarrassing, may remain sitting in one's home a
whole hour merely because they are embarrased to leave: so
perhaps it is the case with such a clergyman, that he, after
having been embarrassed to mount up to the solemn place, is
now embarrassed to say Amen and go down again. But in any
case, the sermon which really begins where the Amen should
be said, like the visit which begins when the moment has come
when it properly should end, are both examples of fortuitous
length, the sign of which is the negative category, *beginning
when one should stop.*

On Authority and Revelation, p. 97 (*Papirer*, VII B 235)

The Man Who Walked Backwards

*Why do inconsistent behaviors so often accompany
exorbitant professions of good intentions?*

When a man turns his back upon someone and walks away,
it is so easy to see that he walks away, but when a man hits
upon a method of turning his face towards the one he is walking away from, hits upon a method of walking backwards
while with appearance and glance and salutations he greets
the person, giving assurances again and again that he is
coming immediately, or incessantly saying "Here I am"—
although he gets farther and farther away by walking backwards—then it is not so easy to become aware. And so it is with
the one who, rich in good intentions and quick to promise,
retreats backwards farther and farther from the good. With
the help of intentions and promises he maintains an orientation towards the good, he is turned towards the good, and with
this orientation towards the good he moves backwards farther
and farther away from it. With every renewed intention and
promise it seems as if he takes a step forward, and yet he not
only remains standing still but really takes a step backward.
The intention taken in vain, the unfulfilled promise leaves a
residue of despondency, dejection, which perhaps soon again
flares up in more passionate protestations of intention, which
leave behind only greater languor. As a drunkard constantly
requires stronger and stronger stimulation—in order to become intoxicated, likewise the one who has fallen into intentions and promises constantly requires more and more stimulation—in order to walk backward.

Works of Love, p. 102 (*SV* XII 95-96)

The August Holiday

To what shall we compare the conceit of modernity that hungers for instant recognition prior to any actual achievement?

The present is the age of anticipation when even recognition is received in advance. No one is satisfied with doing something definite, every one wants to feel flattered by reflection with the illusion of having discovered at the very least a new continent. Like a young man who decides to work for his examination in all earnest from September 1st, and in order to strengthen his resolution decides to take a holiday during August, so the present generation seems—though this is decidedly more difficult to understand—to have made a solemn resolution that the next generation should set to work seriously, and in order to avoid disturbing or delaying the next generation, the present attends to—the banquets. Only there is a difference: the young man understands himself in the light-heartedness of youth, whereas our generation is serious—even at banquets.

The Present Age, p. 36 (*SV* XIV 66)

Kernels and Shells

To what may the relation of God and the world be compared?

If two men were to eat nuts together, and the one liked only the shell, the other only the kernel, one may say that they match one another well. What the world rejects, casts away,

despises, namely, the sacrificed man, the kernel—precisely upon that God sets the greatest store, and treasures it with greater zeal than does the world that which it loves with the greatest passion.[43]

Attack Upon "Christendom," p. 198 (*SV* XIX 212)

The Postponed Answer

What is religion?

When a Greek philosopher was asked to define religion, he asked for time to prepare an answer; when the agreed period had elapsed, he asked for another postponement, and so on. In this way he wished to express symbolically that he regarded the question as unanswerable. This was genuinely in the Greek spirit, beautiful and ingenious. But if he had argued with himself, that since it was so long that he had left the question unanswered, he must now have come nearer to the answer, this would have been a misunderstanding; just as when a debtor remains in debt so long that the debt is finally paid—through having remained so long unpaid.

Johannes Climacus in *Concluding Unscientific Postscript*,
p. 300 (*SV* X 40)

The Imagined Rebellion

Are modern revolutions real or imagined?

A revolutionary age is an age of action; ours is the age of advertisement and publicity. Nothing ever happens but there is immediate publicity everywhere. In the present age a rebellion is, of all things, the most unthinkable. Such an expression of strength would seem ridiculous to the calculating intelligence of our times. On the other hand a political virtuoso might bring off a feat almost as remarkable. He might write a manifesto suggesting a general assembly at which people should decide upon a rebellion, and it would be so carefully worded that even the censor would let it pass. At the meeting itself he would be able to create the impression that his audience had rebelled, after which they would all go quietly home—having spent a very pleasant evening.

The Present Age, p. 35 (*SV* XIV 65)

Luther's Return

Can genuine faith exist without self-sacrificial struggle?

... Assume ... that Luther has risen from his grave. He has been among us, though unrecognized, for several years, has watched the life we lead, has been observant of all the others, and also of me. I assume that one day he addresses me and says, "Are you a believer? Do you have faith?" Everyone who knows me as an author will recognize that I after all am the one who might come out best from such an examination; for I have constantly said, "I have not faith"—like a bird's anxious flight before the approaching tempest, so have I expressed the presentiment of stormy confusion, "I have not faith." This therefore I might say to Luther. I might say, "No, my dear Luther, at least I have shown you this deference, that I declare I have not faith." However, I will not lay stress upon this; but as all the others call themselves Christians and believers, I also will say, "Yes, I am a believer," for otherwise I shall be throwing no light upon the matter I want to see illuminated. So I answer, "Yes, I am a believer." "How is that?" replies Luther, "for I have not noticed anything in you, and yet I have watched your life; and you know, faith is a perturbing thing. To what effect has faith, which you say you have, perturbed you? Where have you witnessed for the truth, and where against the untruth? What sacrifices have you made, what persecutions have you endured for Christianity? And at home in the family life, how has your self-sacrifice and ab-negation been observable?" My reply: "I can protest to you that I have faith." "Protest, protest—what sort of talk is that? With respect to having faith, no protestation is needed, if one has it (for faith is a perturbing thing which is at once observ-able), and no protestation is of any avail, if one does not have it." "Yes, but if only you will believe me, I can protest as solemnly as possible. . . ." "Bah, an end to this nonsense! What avails your protestation?" "Yes, but if you would read some of my books, you will see how I describe faith, so I know therefore that I must have it." "I believe the fellow is mad! If it is true that you know how to describe faith, it only proves that you are a poet, and if you can do it well, it proves that you are a good poet; but this is very far from proving that you are a believer. Perhaps you can also weep in describing faith, that would prove then that you are a good actor."

For Self-Examination, pp. 42-43 (*SV* XVII 62-63)

The Letter

Are there limitations in viewing the scriptures as an object of literary-historical investigation?

Think of a lover who has now received a letter from his beloved—as precious as this letter is to the lover, just so precious to you, I assume, is God's Word; in the way the lover reads this letter, just so, I assume, do you read God's Word and conceive that God's Word ought to be read.

But perhaps you will say, "Yes, but the Holy Scripture is written in a foreign tongue." It is indeed more properly the learned who have the obligation to read the Holy Scriptures in the original tongues; but if you do insist, if you too would stick to it that you must read the Holy Scriptures in the original tongues—all right, we can very well retain the picture of the lover, only we add a little qualification to it.

I assume then that this letter from the beloved was written in a language which the lover did not understand; and there is no one at hand who can translate it for him, and perhaps he did not even desire any aid of that sort, which would initiate a third person into his secrets. What does he do? He takes a dictionary and sits down to spell out the letter, looking up every word so as to get at the translation. Let us suppose that while he is sitting employed in this labor there comes in an acquaintance of his. The friend knows that he has received this letter, and, looking at the table and seeing it lying there, exclaims, "Oho! There you sit reading the letter you got from your lady-love." What do you think the other will say? He replies, "Are you out of your senses? Is this what you call reading a letter from a lady-love? No, my friend, I sit here toiling and drudging to make a translation of it by the help of the dictionary; at times I am on the point of bursting with impatience, the blood rushes to my head so that I want to fling the dictionary down on the floor—and that's what you call reading! You are mocking me. No, thank God, I shall soon be through with the translation, and then, ah, then I shall get to the point of reading the letter from my lady-love—that is an entirely different thing.—But to whom am I speaking . . . . . stupid man, get out of my sight, I don't want to look at you. Oh, that you could think of insulting my lady-love and me by speaking of this as reading her letter! Yet stay, stay, it is only a jest on my part; indeed I should be glad to have you stay, but honestly I have no time, there still remains something to translate, and I am so impatient to get to the point of reading—therefore don't be angry, but go away so that I may finish."

Thus the lover made a distinction between reading and reading, between reading with the dictionary and reading the letter from his lady-love. The blood rushes to his head for impatience while he sits and conjures out the meaning with the dictionary; he is furious with his friend for speaking of this erudite reading as a reading of the letter from his lady-love. He regarded all this (if I may so call it) erudite preparation as a necessary evil, that he might get to the point of . . . . . reading the letter from his lady-love.

Let us not dismiss this picture too soon. Let us suppose

that this letter from the lady-love not only contained, as such letters generally do, the declaration of an emotion, but that there was contained in it a desire, something which the beloved desired the lover to do. There was, let us suppose, a great deal required of him, a very great deal, there was good reason, as every third person would say, to hesitate about doing it; but the lover—he was off in a second to accomplish the desire of the beloved. Let us suppose that in the course of time the lovers met, and the lady said, "But my dear, I didn't think of requiring that of you; you must have misunderstood the word or translated it wrong." Do you believe that the lover now would regret that instead of hastening at once to fulfill the desire of his beloved he had not first entertained some misgivings, and then perhaps had obtained a few more dictionaries to help him out, and then had many misgivings, and then perhaps got the word rightly translated, and so was exempted from the task—do you believe that he regrets this misapprehension? Do you believe that he is less in favor with the beloved? Take the case of a child, one whom we might well call a clever and diligent pupil. When the teacher had appointed the lesson for the next day he says, "Let me see to-morrow that you know your lesson well." This made a deep impression upon our clever pupil. He comes home from school and at once sets to work. But he had not heard quite exactly how far the lesson extended. What does he do? It was this exhortation of the teacher which impressed him, and he reads double the amount actually required of him, as it afterwards proved. Do you believe that the teacher will be the less pleased with him because he can recite admirably a lesson double the prescribed length? Imagine another pupil. He also had heard the teacher's exhortation; nor had he heard exactly how far the lesson extended. Then when he came home he said, "First I have got to find out how much I have to study." So he went to one of his companions, then to another, he was not at home at all, on the contrary he fell to chatting with an elder brother of his—and then at last he came home, and the time for study was past, and he got nothing at all read. . . .

Think now of God's Word. When you read God's Word eruditely—we do not disparage erudition, far from it—but remember that when you read God's word eruditely, with a dictionary, &c., you are not reading God's Word—remember the lover who said, "This is not to read the letter from the beloved." If you are a learned man, then take care lest with all your erudite reading (which is not reading God's Word) you forget perchance to read God's Word. If you are not learned—ah, envy the other man not, rejoice that you can at once get to the point of reading God's Word! And if there is a desire, a commandment, an order, then (remember the lover!), then be off at once to do acordingly. "But," you perhaps would say, "there are so many obscure passages in the Holy Scriptures, whole books which are almost riddles." To this I would reply: "I see no need of considering this objection unless it comes from one whose life gives expression to the fact that he has punctually complied with all the passages which are easy to understand." Is this the case with you? Yet thus it is the lover would deal with the letter; if there were obscure passages, but also clearly expressed desires, he would say, "I must at once comply with the desire, then I will see what can be made of the obscure passages. Oh, but how could I sit down to puzzle over the obscure passages and leave the desire unfulfilled, the desire which I clearly understood?" That is to say: When you read God's Word, it is not the obscure passages which impose a duty upon you, but that which you understand and with that you must instantly comply. If there were only a single passage you did understand in Holy Scripture—well, the first thing is to do that; but you do not first have to sit down and puzzle over the obscure passages. God's Word is given in order that you shall act in accordance with it, not in order that you shall practice the art of interpreting obscure passages.

. . . Oh, my friend, was the lady-love displeased that the lover had been doing too much? and what would she say about entertaining such a fear? She would say, "He who entertains such a fear of doing too much is not really reading the letter from his beloved." And so I would say: "He does not read God's Word."

Let us not even yet dismiss this picture of the lover and his letter. While he was busily engaged translating with the aid of a dictionary, he was disturbed by the visit of an acquaintance. He became impatient—"But," he likely would have said, "that was only because I was retarded in my work, for otherwise it would have been of no importance. I wasn't reading the letter then. Of course, if someone had come to see me when I was reading the letter, it would have been quite another matter—that would have been a disturbance. Against that danger, however, I shall ensure myself; before beginning a thing like that I lock my door tight and am not at home. For I would be alone with the letter, alone and undisturbed; if I am not alone, I am not reading the letter from the beloved!" ...

And so it is with God's Word: he who is not alone with God's Word is not reading God's Word.

For Self-Examination, pp. 51-55 (*SV* XVII 69-73)

The Creation of Woman

*How shall we account for the captivating power and
mystery of feminine existence?*

It is my joy that the female sex, far from being more imperfect
than man, is on the contrary the most perfect. However I will
clothe my speech in a myth. . . .

"Originally there was one sex, that of the man—so the
Greeks report. Gloriously endowed was he, so that he reflected
honor upon the gods who created him, so gloriously endowed
that the gods were in the position in which a poet sometimes
finds himself when he has expended all his forces upon a
poetic creation: they became envious of man. Yea, what was
worse, they feared him, lest he might bow unwillingly to their
yoke. They feared, though it was without reason, that he might
cause heaven itself to totter. So then they had conjured up a
power they hardly thought themselves capable of curbing.
Then there was concern and commotion in the council of the
gods. Much had they lavished upon the creation of man, that
was magnanimous; now everything must be risked, for everything was at stake, this was self-defense. So thought the gods.
And it was impossible to revoke him, as a poet may revoke
his thought. By force he could not be compelled, or else the
gods themselves might have compelled him, but it was precisely about this they had misgivings. He must then be taken
captive and compelled by a power which was weaker than his
own and yet stronger, strong enough to compel. What a marvelous power that must be! Necessity, however, teaches the
gods to surpass themselves in inventiveness. They sought and
pondered and found. This power was woman, the miracle of
creation even in the eyes of the gods a greater miracle than
man, a discovery for which the gods in their naiveté could not

help patting themselves on the back. What more can be said in honor of her than that she should be able to do what even the gods did not think themselves capable of doing, what more can be said than that she was able? How marvelous she must be to be capable of it! This was a ruse of the gods. Cunningly the enchantress was fashioned; the very instant she had enchanted man she transformed herself and held him captive in all the prolixities of finiteness. This is what the gods wanted. But what can be more delicious, more pleasurable, more enchanting, than this which the gods as they were fighting for their own power devised as the only thing that could decoy man? And verily it is so, for woman is the unique and the most seductive power in heaven and on earth. In this comparison man is something exceedingly imperfect.

"And the ruse of the gods succeeded. However, it did not always succeed. In every generation there were some men, individuals, who became aware of the deception. They perceived her loveliness, it is true, more than did any of the others, but they had an inkling what it was all about. These are what I call erotics, and I reckon myself among them; men call them seducers, woman has no name for them, such a type is for her unmentionable. These erotics are the fortunate ones. They live more luxuriously than the gods, for they eat constantly only that which is more precious than ambrosia and drink what is more delicious than nectar; they dine upon the most seductive fancy which issued from the most artful thought of the gods, they dine constantly upon bait. Oh, luxury beyond compare! Oh, blissful mode of living! They dine constantly upon bait—and are never caught. The other men set to and eat bait as the vulgar eat caviar, and are caught. Only the erotic knows how to appreciate bait, to appreciate it infinitely. Woman divines this, and hence there is a secret understanding between him and her. . . .

"Thus the gods fashioned her, delicate and ethereal as the mists of a summer's night and yet plump like a ripened fruit, light as a bird in spite of the fact that she carried a world of craving, light because the play of forces is unified at the invisible center of a negative relationship in which she is related to herself, slim of stature, designed with definite proportions and yet to the eye seeming to swell with the wavelines of beauty, complete and yet as if only now she were finished, cooling, delicious, refreshing as new-fallen snow, blushing with serene transparency, happy as a jest which causes one to forget everything, tranquilizing as the goal whereunto desire tends, satisfying by being herself the incitement of desire. And this is what the gods had counted upon, that man upon catching sight of her should be amazed as one who gets a sight of himself in the glass, and yet again as if he were familiar with this sight, amazed as one who sees himself reflected in perfection, amazed as one who sees what he never had an inkling of and yet sees, as it appears to him, what must necessarily have occurred to him, what is a necessary part of existence, and yet sees this as the riddle of existence."

Johannes the Seducer[44] in *Stages on Life's Way*,
pp. 83-85 (*SV* VII 70-72)

The Early Finish

Is the task of becoming a self ever completed?

When in a written examination the youth are allotted four hours to develop a theme, then it is neither here nor there if an individual student happens to finish before the time is up, or uses the entire time. Here, therefore, the task is one thing, the time another. But when the time itself is the task, it becomes a fault to finish before the time has transpired. Suppose a man were assigned the task of entertaining himself for an entire day, and he finishes this task of self-entertainment as early as noon: then his celerity would not be meritorious. So also when life constitutes the task. To be finished with life before life has finished with one, is precisely not to have finished the task.[45]

Johannes Climacus in *Concluding Unscientific Postscript*,
pp. 146-47 (*SV* IX 137)

The Salmon Crisis

Should sentiment be checked and resisted?

In itself, salmon is a great delicacy; but too much of it is harmful, since it taxes the digestion. At one time when a very large catch of salmon had been brought to Hamburg, the police ordered that a householder should give his servants only one meal a week of salmon. One could wish for a similar police order against sentimentality.

"A" in *Either/Or*, I, p. 41 (*SV* II 43)

The Society to Counteract Wine Drinking

*How shall we sort out the conflict between renunciation
and remuneration in the religious sphere?*

Imagine that a society was formed for the purpose of counter-
acting the drinking of wine.

To that end the director of the society thought it expedient
to engage a number of men who as emissaries, speakers, call
them "priests," could travel through the whole land, working
to win men and persuade them to join the society.

"But," said the director at the meeting when the thing was
decided, "to economize on the priests doesn't do a damn bit of
good, to require them not to drink wine leads to nothing, all
we get out of that is the watery and fasting talk which doesn't
fill anybody with enthusiasm for joining our association. No,
we must not economize on the priest, he must have his bottle
of wine every day, and in proportion to his zeal something
extra, so that he may have a liking for his work, and with
warmth, vigor, the whole power of conviction, he will carry
people away, so that they will enter our society in countless
numbers."

Suppose that all of them became, not members of the society,
but priests in the service of this society.

So it is with Christianity and the State. Christianity, the
teaching about renunciation, about heterogeneity to this world,
a teaching which issues no checks except those payable in another world, this teaching the State wants to have introduced.
"But," says the State, "to economize on the priests really
doesn't do any good, all we get out of it is a kind of fasting
and waterish something which wins nobody for the teaching
but rather scares them all away. No, the priest must be re-
munerated in such a way, his life arranged in such a way, that

he can find pleasure, both for himself and with his family, in preaching this doctrine. Thus there can be hope for winning men for the renunciation of the earthly; for the priest will be in the mood to describe to men with warmth, vigor, the whole power of conviction, how blessed this renunciation and suffering is, how blessed it is to get checks payable only in another world, that it is [listen to him!] blessed, blessed, blessed! . . ."

Attack Upon "Christendom," p. 112 (*SV* XIX 125-26)

The Quiet Despair

How may the despair of one collude quietly with the despair of another?

When Swift was old he was taken into the madhouse he himself had founded in his youth. There, it is related, he often stood before a mirror with the persistence of a vain and wanton woman, though not exactly with her thoughts. He looked at himself and said: "Poor old man!"

There was once a father and a son. A son is like a mirror in which the father beholds himself, and for the son the father too is like a mirror in which he beholds himself in the time to come. However, they rarely regarded one another in this way, for their daily intercourse was characterized by the cheerfulness of gay and lively conversation. It happened only a few times that the father came to a stop, stood before the son with a sorrowful countenance, looked at him steadily and said: "Poor child, you are going into a quiet despair." True as this saying was, nothing was ever said to indicate how it was to be understood. And the father believed that he was to blame for the son's melancholy, and the son believed that he was the occasion of the father's sorrow—but they never exchanged a word on this subject.

87

Then the father died, and the son saw much, experienced much, and was tried in manifold temptations; but infinitely inventive as love is, longing and the sense of loss taught him, not indeed to wrest from the silence of eternity a communication, but to imitate the father's voice so perfectly that he was content with the likeness. So he did not look at himself in a mirror like the aged Swift, for the mirror was no longer there; but in loneliness he comforted himself by hearing the father's voice: "Poor child, thou art going into a quiet despair." For the father was the only one who had understood him, and yet he did not know in fact whether he had understood him; and the father was the only confidant he had had, but the confidence was of such a sort that it remained the same whether the father lived or died.[46]

Quidam in *Stages on Life's Way*, pp. 191-92 (*SV* VIII 23)

The Prompter

*What goes on between the speaker and the hearer
in a genuine edifying discourse?*

It is so on the stage, as you know well enough, that someone
sits and prompts by whispers; [he is hidden;][47] he is the in-
conspicuous one; he is and wishes to be overlooked. But then
there is another, he strides out prominently, he draws every eye
to himself. For that reason he has been given his name, that is:
actor. He impersonates a distinct individual. In the skillful
sense of this illusory art, each word becomes true when em-
bodied in him, true through him—and yet he is told what he
shall say by the hidden one that sits and whispers. No one is
so foolish as to regard the prompter as more important than
the actor.

Now forget this light talk about art. Alas, in regard to things
spiritual, the foolishness of many is this, that they in the
secular sense look upon the speaker as an actor, and the listeners as theatergoers who are to pass judgment upon the artist.
But the speaker is not the actor—not in the remotest sense. No,
the speaker is the prompter. There are no mere theatergoers
present, for each listener will be looking into his own heart.
The stage is eternity, and the listener, if he is the true listener
(and if he is not, he is at fault) stands before God during the
talk. The prompter whispers to the actor what he is to say, but
the actor's repetition of it is the main concern—is the solemn
charm of the art. The speaker whispers the word to the listeners. But the main concern is earnestness: that the listeners by
themselves, with themselves, and to themselves, in the silence
before God, may speak with the help of this address.

The address is not given for the speaker's sake, in order
that men may praise or blame him. The listener's repetition of

it is what is aimed at. If the speaker has the responsibility for what he whispers, then the listener has an equally great responsibility not to fall short in his task. In the theater, the play is staged before an audience who are called theatergoers; but at the devotional address, God himself is present. In the most earnest sense, God is the critical theatergoer, who looks on to see how the lines are spoken and how they are listened to: hence here the customary audience is wanting. The speaker is then the prompter, and the listener stands openly before God. The listener, if I may say so, is the actor, who in all truth acts before God.

Purity of Heart, pp. 180-81 (*SV* XI 114-15)

The Dapper *Privatdocent*

What is the position of speculative philosophy in relation to Christianity?

Suppose . . . there came a man who had to say: "I have not indeed believed, but so much have I honored Christianity that I have employed every hour of my life in pondering it." Or suppose there came one of whom the accuser had to say: "He has persecuted the Christians," and the accused replied: "Aye, I admit it; Christianity has set my soul aflame, and I have had no other ambition than to root it from the earth, precisely because I perceived its tremendous power." Or suppose there came another, of whom the accuser would have to say: "He has abjured Christianity," and the accused replied: "Aye, it is true; for I saw that Christianity was such a power that if I gave it a little finger it would take the whole man, and I felt that I could not belong to it wholly." But then suppose there finally came a dapper *Privatdocent* with light and nimble steps, who spoke as follows: "I am not like these three; I have not only believed, but I have even explained Christianity, and shown that as it was expounded by the Apostles and appropriated in the early centuries it was only to a certain degree true; but that now, through the interpretation of speculative philosophy it has become the true truth, whence I must ask for a suitable reward on account of my services to Christianity." Which of these four must be regarded as in the most terrible position? It is just possible that Christianity is the truth; suppose that now when its ungrateful children desire to have it declared incompetent, and placed under the guardianship of speculative philosophy, like the Greek poet whose children also demanded that the aged parent be placed under a guardian, but who astonished the judges and the people by writing one of his most beautiful tragedies as a sign that he was still in the full possession of his faculties—suppose that Christianity thus arose with renewed vigor: there would be no one else whose position would become as embarrassing as the position of the *Privatdocents*.

Johannes Climacus in *Concluding Unscientific Postscript*,
pp. 207-08 (*SV* IX 193-94)

The Cellar Tenant

*To what shall we compare our persistent spiritual
self-rejection?*

In case one were to think of a house, consisting of cellar,
ground-floor and *premier étage*, so tenanted, or rather so arranged, that it was planned for a distinction of rank between
the dwellers on the several floors; and in case one were to make
a comparison between such a house and what it is to be a
man—then unfortunately this is the sorry and ludicrous condition of the majority of men, that in their own house they
prefer to live in the cellar. The soulish-bodily synthesis in every
man is planned with a view to being spirit, such is the building; but the man prefers to dwell in the cellar, that is, in the
determinants of sensuousness. And not only does he prefer to
dwell in the cellar; no, he loves that to such a degree that he
becomes furious if anyone would propose to him to occupy the
bel étage which stands empty at his disposition—for in fact he
is dwelling in his own house.

Anti-Climacus in *The Sickness unto Death*,
p. 176 (*SV* XV 100)

The Lifelong Schooling

How much time may we justifiably spend on the education of the human spirit?

The lowest forms of animals are born in one moment and die almost in the same moment; the lower animals grow very rapidly. The human being grows the slowest of all created beings, and thereby he confirms the well-informed man in believing that man is the noblest creation. And we also speak in the same way about education. He who is merely destined to serve in a humble capacity goes to school only a short time. But the one who is destined for something higher, must go to school for a long time. Consequently, the length of the educational period has a direct relationship to the significance of that which one is to become. If, therefore, the school of suffering lasts through an entire lifetime, then this simply proves that this school must train for the highest, moreover, that it is the only one which does train for eternity, for no other time of schooling lasts so long. Certainly if a temporal wisdom were to think that a man should spend his whole life in going to school, then the learner might rightly become impatient and say: "When am I going to get any good from what I have learned in this school!" Only eternity can justify to itself and to the learner the making of his whole life into a period of schooling. But if eternity is to keep the school, then it must also become the most distinguished school, but the most distinguished school is precisely the one which lasts longest. As a teacher usually says to the youthful student, who is even now finding the time of schooling too long, "Now, just don't get impatient, you have a long life before you"—so eternity speaks with more reason and more reliability to the sufferer: "Just wait, do not become impatient, there is indeed plenty of time, there is, you know, eternity."

The Gospel of Suffering, pp. 60-61 (*SV* XI 241-42)

The Diagnosis

Just how far can the therapeutic professionals go in objectively analyzing the demonic?

The demoniacal has been regarded therapeutically. As a matter of course: "*Mit Pulver und mit Pillen*" [Take my powder and my pills]—and then clysters![48] Then the apothecary and the doctor put their heads together. The patient has been isolated so that the others might not be afraid. In our courageous age one does not say to a patient that he will die, one does not dare to call the priest for fear the patient may die of fright, one does not dare to say to the patient that the same day a man died of the same illness. The patient was isolated, compassion made inquiries about him, the physician promised to issue as soon as possible a tabulated statistical statement in order to determine the average. And when one has the average, everything is explained. The therapeutic way of viewing the case regards the phenomenon as purely physical and somatic, and it does as physicians often do, especially in Hoffman's novels —it takes its pinch of snuff and says, "This is a serious case."

Vigilius Haufniensis in *The Concept of Dread*,
p. 108 (*SV* VI 205)

The Lash of the Royal Coachman

How does one obtain an impression of the absolute?

If you were to ask a peasant, a cabman, a postilion, a livery-man, "What does the coachman use the whip for?" you shall get the same reply from them all: "Of course it is to make the horse go." Ask the King's coachman, "What does a coachman use the whip for?" and you shall hear him reply, "Principally, it is used to make the horses stand still." This is the distinction between being a simple driver and a good driver. Now further. Have you ever observed how the King's coachman comports himself? Or if you have not observed that, then let me describe it to you. He sits high on his box, and just because he sits so high he has the horses all the more under his control. In certain circumstances, however, he does not consider this enough. He raises himself in his seat, concentrating all his physical force in the muscular arm which wields the whip—then one lash falls; it was frightful. Generally one lash is enough, but sometimes the horse makes a desperate plunge—one lash more. That suffices. He sits down. But the horse? First a tremor passes through its whole body, actually it seems as if this fiery, powerful creature were hardly able to support itself upon its legs; that is the first effect, it is not so much the pain that makes it tremble as the fact that the coachman—as only the King's coachman can—has wholly concentrated himself in giving emphasis to the lash, so that the horse is aware (not so much by reason of the pain as by something else) who it is that delivers the lash. Then this tremor decreases, there is left now only a slight shudder, but it is as if every muscle, every fibre quivered. Now this is over—now the horse stands still, absolutely still. What was this? It got the impression of the absolute, hence it is absolutely still. When a horse which the

96

royal coachman drives stands still, it is not at all the same thing as when a cab-horse stands still, for in the latter case this means merely that it is not going, and there is no art required for that; whereas in the first case, to stand still is an act, an effort, the most strenuous effort, and also the horse's highest art, and it stands absolutely still.

How shall I describe this? Let me use another figure which comes to the same thing. In daily speech we talk in a way about its being still weather, though it perfectly well may be blowing a little, or there may be at least a slight breeze, it is only what in a way we call still weather. But have you never noticed another sort of stillness? Just before a thunder-storm comes up there sometimes is such a stillness; it is of a different sort entirely; not a leaf stirs, not a breath of air, it is as though all nature stood still, although in fact a slight, almost imperceptible shudder passes through everything. What does the absolute stillness of this imperceptible shudder signify? It signifies that the absolute is expected, the thunder-storm—and the horse's absolute stillness, that was after having got the impression of the absolute.

Judge for Yourselves!, pp. 123-24 (*SV* XVII 141-42)

The Wooden Horse

*How does interior suffering experience its being grossly
misunderstood by outsiders?*

In old times the army employed a very cruel punishment, that
of riding a wooden horse. The unfortunate man was held
down by weights on a wooden horse with a very sharp back.
One time when this punishment was put in execution and the
culprit was groaning with pain, up came a peasant who walked
on the rampart and stopped to look at the drillground where
the culprit was undergoing his punishment. Desperate with
pain and irritated by the sight of such a blockhead, the unfortunate man shouted at him: "What are you staring at?"
But the peasant replied, "If you can't bear to have anybody
look at you, then you can ride around by another street." And
just as that riding culprit was riding, so is the current year
running with me.

Quidam in *Stages on Life's Way*, p. 206 (*SV* VIII 38)

The Girl of Sixteen and the Man of Twenty-five

What existence is the happiest?

What is the happiest existence? It is that of a young girl of sixteen years when she, pure and innocent, possesses nothing, not a chest of drawers or a pedestal, but has to make use of the lowest drawer of her mother's escritoire to keep all her magnificence: the confirmation dress and a prayer-book! Happy the man who possesses no more than he is content to put in the next drawer.

What existence is the happiest? It is that of a young girl of sixteen years, pure and innocent, who indeed can dance but goes to a ball only twice a year!

What is the happiest existence? It is that of a young girl when, sixteen summers old, pure and innocent, she sits diligently at her work and yet finds time to glance sidewise at him, at him who possesses nothing, not a chest of drawers, not a pedestal, but is only a partner in the same wardrobe, and yet has an entirely different explanation of the case, for in her he possesses the whole world, in spite of the fact that she possesses nothing.

And who then is the most unhappy? It is that rich young man twenty-five winters old who dwells opposite.

When one is sixteen summers old and the other sixteen winters old, are they not equally old? Ah, no! How is that, is not the time identical when it is identical? Ah, no! The time is not identical.

Quidam in *Stages on Life's Way*, pp. 246-47 (*SV* VIII 79)

Nebuchadnezzar

*How is human pride and power changed when it stands
in awe of the power and majesty of God?*

1. Recollections of my life when I was a beast and ate grass.
I, Nebuchadnezzar, to all peoples and tongues.

2. Was not Babel the great city, the greatest of all the cities
of the nations? I, I Nebuchadnezzar, have built it.

3. No city was so renowned as Babel, and no king so renowned through Babel, the glory of my majesty.

4. My royal house was visible unto the ends of the earth,
and my wisdom was like a dark riddle which none of the wise
men could explain.

5. So they could not tell what it was I had dreamed.

6. And the word came to me that I should be transformed
and become like a beast which eateth the grass of the field
while seven seasons changed over me.

7. Then I assembled all my princes with their armies and
disposed that I should be forewarned when the enemy came
as the word indicated.

8. But no one dared approach proud Babel, and I said, "Is
not this proud Babel which I have built?"

9. Now there was heard a voice suddenly, and I was transformed as quickly as a woman changeth color.

10. Grass was my food, and dew fell upon me, and no one
knew me who I was.

11. But I knew Babel and cried, "Is not this Babel?" But no
one heeded my word, for when it sounded it was like the
bellowing of a beast.

12. My thoughts terrified me, my thoughts in my mind, for
my mouth was bound, and no one could perceive anything
but a voice in likeness as a beast's.

13. And I thought, Who is that Mighty One, the Lord, the Lord, whose wisdom is like the darkness of the night, and like the deep sea unfathomable?

14. Yea, like a dream which He alone understandeth, and the interpretation of which He hath not delivered into any man's power, when suddenly He is upon one and holds one in His powerful arms.

15. No one knoweth where this Mighty One dwelleth, no one could point and say, "Behold, here is His throne," so that one could travel through the land till it was said, "Behold, here is the confine of His dominion."

16. For He dwelleth not on the confines of my kingdom as my neighbor, neither from the uttermost sea unto the confines of my kingdom like a bulwark round about.

17. And neither doth He dwell in His Temple, for I, I Nebuchadnezzar, have taken His vessels of gold and vessels of silver, and have laid His Temple waste.

18. And no one knoweth anything of Him, who was His father, and how He acquired His power, and who taught Him the secret of His might.

19. And He hath no counselors, that one might buy His secret for gold; no one to whom He says, "What shall I do?" and no one who says to Him, "What doest thou?"

20. Spies He has not, to spy after the opportunity when one might catch Him; for He doth not say, "Tomorrow," but He saith, "Today."

21. For He maketh no preparations like a man, and His preparations give the enemy no respite; for He saith, "Let it be done," and it cometh to pass.

22. He sitteth still and speaketh with Himself, one knoweth not that He is present until it cometh to pass.

23. This hath He done against me. He aimeth not like the bowman, so that one might flee from His arrow; He speaketh with Himself, and it is done.

24. In His hand the brain of kings is like wax in the smelting oven, and their potency is like a feather when He weigheth it.

25. And yet He dwelleth not on earth as the Mighty One, that He might take from me Babel and leave me a small residue, or that He might take from me all and be the Mighty One in Babel.

26. So did I think in the secrecy of my mind, when no one knew me, and my thoughts terrified me, that the Lord, the Lord was such as that.

27. But when the seven years were past I became again Nebuchadnezzar.

28. And I called together all the wise men that they might explain to me the secret of that power, and how I had become a beast of the field.

29. And they all fell down upon their faces and said, "Great Nebuchadnezzar, this is an imagination, an evil dream! Who could be capable of doing this to thee?"

30. But my wrath was kindled against the wise men in the whole land, and I had them cut down in their folly.

31. For the Lord, the Lord possesseth all might, as no man doth possess it, and I will not envy Him his power, but will laud it and be next to Him, for I have taken His vessels of gold and vessels of silver.

32. Babel is no more the renowned Babel, and I, Nebuchadnezzar, am no more Nebuchadnezzar, and my armies protect me no more, for no one can see the Lord, the Lord, and no one can recognize Him.

33. Though He were to come, and the watchmen were to give warning in vain, because already I should have become like a bird in the tree, or like a fish in the water, known only to the other fish.

34. Therefore I desire no longer to be renowned through Babel, but every seventh year there shall be a festival in the land,

35. A great festival among the people, and it shall be called the Feast of the Transformation.

36. And an astrologer shall be led through the streets and be clad like a beast, and his calculations shall he carry with him, torn to shreds like a bunch of hay.

37. And all the people shall cry, "The Lord, the Lord, the Lord is the Mighty One, and His deed is swift like the leap of the great fish in the sea."

38. For soon my days are told, and my dominion gone like a watch in the night, and I know not whither I go hence,

39. Whether I come to the invisible land in the distance where the Mighty One dwelleth, that I might find grace in His eyes;

40. Whether it be He that taketh from me the breath of life, that I become as a cast-off garment like my predecessors, that he might find delight in me.

41. This have I, I Nebuchadnezzar, made known to all peoples and tongues, and great Babel shall carry out my will.[49]

Quidam in *Stages on Life's Way*, pp. 330-33 (*SV* VIII 165-68)

A Possibility

*What is the strange power of possibility, that it may affect
one's entire life, even if it is only a distant
possibility of an uncertain event?*

Longbridge gets its name from its length, for as a bridge it is
long, though as a road the length of the bridge is not very
considerable, of which one can convince oneself by crossing it.
Then when one is standing on the other side, in Christianshavn, it seems as though the bridge must after all be very
long, for it seems as though one were far, very far away from
Copenhagen. One notices immediately that this town is not a
capital or royal residence, one misses in a sense the noise and
traffic in the streets, one feels as though one were out of one's
element when one is out of the bustle of meeting and parting
and hasting on, in which the most disparate interests assert
for themselves an equal importance, out of the noisy sociality
in which everyone contributes his part to the general hubbub.
At Christianshavn, on the other hand, there prevails a quiet
repose. There people do not seem to be acquainted with the
aims and purposes which prompt the inhabitants of the metropolis to such noisy and busy activity, do not seem to be
acquainted with the diversities which underlie the clamorous
movement of the capital. Here the ground does not move, or
rather shake, beneath one's feet, and one stands as securely as
any stargazer or dowser could wish to stand for the sake of
his observations. One looks about in vain for that social *poscia-
mur*,[50] where it is so easy to go with the others, where every instant one can get rid of oneself, every hour can find a seat in the
omnibus, surrounded on all sides by conductors, where one
feels so deserted and imprisoned in the quietness which iso-
lates, where one cannot get rid of oneself, where on all sides

one is surrounded by nonconductors. In certain quarters there are streets so empty that one can hear one's own footfall. The big warehouses contain nothing and bring in nothing, for though Echo is a very quiet lodger, yet in the way of business and rent no owner is the better for it. In the populous quarters life is far from being extinct, and yet it is so far from being loud that the quiet human murmur suggests to me at least the buzzing of summer out in the country. One becomes sad as soon as one enters Christianshavn, for memory is sad out there among the empty storehouses, and in the overpopulated streets the sight is sad where the eye discovers only an idyl of poverty and wretchedness. One has crossed the salt water to get here, and now one is far, far away, in another and remote world where dwells a race which deals in horseflesh, where in the only square there stands a solitary ruin, ever since that conflagration which did not, as pious superstition recounts in other instances, leave the church standing while it consumed everything else, but consumed the church and left only the prison standing. One is in a poor provincial town where the only reminder of the vicinity of the capital is the presence of suspicious characters and the special vigilance of the police; everything else is just as it is in a provincial town; the quiet hum of humanity, the fact that they all know one another, that there is a shabby fellow who at least every other day does duty as a drunkard, and that there is a lunatic known to everybody, who shifts for himself.

So it is that several years ago there might have been seen at a definite hour of the day at the southern extremity of Water Street a tall, thin man who walked with measured tread back and forth along the pavement. The strangeness of this promenade could scarcely escape anybody's attention, for the distance he traversed was so short that even the uninitiated must observe that he neither was out on business, nor was taking a constitutional like other people. Those who observed him often could discern in his walk a symbol of the power of custom. A sea-captain, accustomed on shipboard to promenade the length of the deck, marks out on land a distance of equal length and walks mechanically back and forth—so did this wayfarer, or bookkeeper, as the people called him. When he had reached the end of the street one observed in him the converse of an electric shock, the tug of custom in him: he came to a halt, swung about, turned his eyes again to the ground, and then marched back, and so on.

He was known naturally in the whole quarter, but in spite of the fact that he was crazy he never was exposed to insult; on the contrary, by the inhabitants of the neighborhood he was treated with a certain deference. This was due in part to his wealth, but also to his beneficence and to his advantageous appearance. His face, it is true, had that monotonous expression so characteristic of a certain sort of lunacy, but the features were fine, his figure erect and handsome, his dress was scrupulous and even elegant. His lunacy was very plainly exhibited only in the forenoon between eleven and twelve o'clock, when he walked out along the paved way between the Børnehus Bridge and the end of the street. The rest of the day he doubtless was dangling after his luckless preoccupation, but his aberration did not show itself in this way. He talked with people, made longer excursions, took an interest in many things; but between eleven and twelve o'clock one could not at any price get him to stop walking, to go on farther, to make a response to a questioner, or even so much as to return a greeting, though at other times he was courtesy itself. Whether this hour had some special significance to him, or whether, as sometimes occurs, he was actuated by a bodily disorder of regular recurrence, I never was able to learn while he was alive, and after his death there was no one from whom I could seek more precise information.

Now although the inhabitants of the neighborhood almost reminded one by their attitude towards him of the behavior of the Indians towards a lunatic, whom they venerated as a wise man, they perhaps privately had conjectures about the cause of his misfortune. It not infrequently happens that a man reputed to be shrewd betrays by such conjectures quite as much disposition to madness, and perhaps more puerility, than any lunatic can be charged with. The so-called shrewd people are often stupid enough to believe everything a madman says, and often stupid enough to believe that everything he says is madness, although no one is more cunning than a lunatic often is in hiding what he wants to hide, and although many a word of a crazy man contains a wisdom which a wise man need not be ashamed of. Hence it is perhaps that the same notion which regards the governance of the universe as being determined by a grain of sand or a mere accident is considered valid in psychology; for it is the same notion when one descries no deeper cause for insanity but regards it as easily explicable by nothing, just as mediocre actors think that to play the part of a drunken man is the easiest job—which only is true when one can be sure of a mediocre audience. The bookkeeper was shielded from ridicule because he was loved, and the conjectures about him were so securely preserved in silence that actually I never heard more than one. Perhaps the neighbors had no more concealed under their silence; that is a view I too can adopt, and I am not disinclined to do so, for fear my obstinate suspicion that they privately had many conjectures should betray in me disposition to puerility. The conjecture was that he had been in love with a queen of Spain; and this obviously was wide of the mark since it did not account for one of the most remarkable traits, his decisive predilection for children. In this way he did a great deal of good, actually consuming his fortune in doing it; hence he was sincerely loved by the poor, and many a poor woman instructed her children to greet the bookkeeper deferentially. But in the morning between eleven and twelve he never responded to a greeting. I have often seen a poor woman pass him with her child and greet him in the most friendly and deferential way, as did the child too, but he did not look up. When the poor woman had gone by I saw her toss her head. The situation was touching, for his benefactions were in a very characteristic and curious sense entirely gratis. The pawnshop takes six per cent on a loan, and many a rich, many a fortunate, many a mighty man, and many a middleman between them and the poor, will sometimes take usury on the gift, but in the case of the bookkeeper a poor woman was not tempted to be envious of him, or dejected because of her wretchedness, or cowed by the poor-rates, which the poor do not pay in money but work out by a bended back and a mortified soul, for she had the feeling that her "noble and generous benefactor" (to use the expression of the poor) was more unfortunate than she—than she who got from the bookkeeper the money she had need of.

But he was not interested in children merely as an opportunity for doing good; no, he was interested in the children themselves, and that in a very singular way. The moment he saw a child, at any time but the hour between eleven and twelve, the monotonous expression of his face became mobile and reflected a great variety of moods, he made up to the child, engaged it in conversation, and all the while regarded it with such close attention that he might have been an artist who painted children's faces only.[51]

This is what one saw in the street, but one who saw him in his apartment might marvel still more. One frequently gets an entirely different impression of a person seeing him in his home and in his chamber than when one sees him elsewhere. And this is not true only of alchemists and others who busy themselves with occult arts and sciences, or of astrologers, like Dapsul von Zabelthau,[52] who in his sitting-room looks like other people, but seated in his observatory has a high peaked cap on his head, a mantle of gray callimanco, a long white beard, and talks with a dissembled voice so that his own daughter cannot recognize him but takes him for a bugaboo. Ah, one not infrequently discovers an entirely different sort of change when one sees a person in his home or his chamber, and then compares him as he here appears to be with what he appears to be in public life. Such was not the case with the bookkeeper, and one only saw with astonishment how serious his interest in children actually was. He had collected a considerable library, but all the books had to do with physiology. Among them were to be found the most costly copper engravings, and along with them whole series of his own drawings, including faces drawn with the precision of portraits, then a row of faces connected with one original in a sequence which showed how the likeness constantly grew less, though a trace of it always remained; there were faces executed in accordance with mathematical formulae, others which illustrated by a few clear lines how a slight alteration in the proportions completely altered the total impression; there were faces constructed according to physiological observations, and these in turn were checked by other faces sketched in accordance with a hypothetical assumption. In all of these what interested him particularly were the similarities attributable to family relationship in successive generations as seen from the point of view of physiology, psychology, and pathology. It is perhaps to be regretted that his works never saw the light of day; for it is true he was a lunatic, as I learned on closer acquaintance, but a lunatic is by no means the worst observer when his fixed idea becomes an instinct for prying things out. A curiously interested observer sees a great deal, a scientifically interested observer is worthy of all honor, an anxiously interested observer sees what others do not see, but a crazy observer sees perhaps most, his observation is more intense and more persistent, just as the senses of certain animals are sharper than those of man. Only it goes without saying that his observations must be verified.

When he was thus occupied with his passionate investigation (which generally speaking was at all times except between the hours of eleven and twelve) many people would suppose that he was not crazy, although it was precisely then his lunacy permeated him most completely. And as underlying every scientific investigation, there is an x which has to be sought for, or (regarded from another side) as the thing which prompts the scientific investigation, which is an eternal presumption seeking to corroborate its certainty by observation; just so did his anxious passion have an x which it sought, a law which would determine precisely the degree of resemblance in racial inheritance and thus enable one to reach an exact conclusion; and so too did he have a presumption to which his imagination lent a dolorous certainty that this discovery would confirm some dolorous fact concerning himself.

He was the son of a subordinate government employee living in modest circumstances. At an early age he got a position with one of the richest merchants. Quiet, retiring, rather shy and embarrassed, he attended to his business with an intelligence and punctuality which soon led the head of the house to discover in him a very useful man. He employed his leisure time in reading, in studying foreign languages, in developing his decided talent for drawing, and in making a daily visit to the house of his parents, where he was the only child. So he lived on without knowledge of the world. He was employed as accountant, and soon he was in receipt of a considerable salary. If it be true, as the Englishman says, that money makes virtue, it is certain also that money makes vice. However, the young man was not tempted, but as year after year went by he became more and more a stranger to the world. He himself hardly noticed this because his time was always fully occupied. Only once did a presentiment of it dawn upon his soul, he became a stranger to himself, or was like one who pulls himself up and vaguely recalls something he must have forgotten, though without being able to comprehend what it was. And something indeed he had forgotten, for he had forgotten to be young and to let his heart delight itself in the manner of youth before the days of youth were past.

Then he became acquainted with a couple of clerks who were men of the world. They soon were aware of his shy embarrassment but had so much respect for his ability and knowledge that they never did anything to make him conscious of his lack. Sometimes they invited him to take part with them in a little gaiety, in short excursions, or at the theater. He did it and liked it. His companions on the other hand were doubtless none the worse for his company, for his shyness put a wholesome check upon their merriment, so that it did not become wanton, and his purity imparted to their very amusements a nobler character than perhaps they were accustomed to. But shyness is not a power able to maintain its position and assert itself, and whether it was that the sadness which sometimes seized a man unacquainted with the world then revolted against him, or whatever other cause there may have been, at all events an excursion in the forest ended with an unusually sumptuous dinner party.[53] Frolicsome as the two clerks already were, his shyness became only an incentive to them, and the painful sense of it on his part became an incentive to him, which had a more and more powerful effect the more they were inflamed by wine. Then the others led him with them, and in his over-excitement he became an entirely different man—and he was in bad company. So then they visited one of those places where, strangely enough, one gives money for a woman's despicableness. What occurred there even he himself did not know.[54]

The following day he was out of sorts and dispirited; sleep had obliterated the impression, yet he remembered enough not to want to seek again the society of these friends, whether it was reputable or evil society. If he had been diligent before, he now became all the more so, and the pain he felt for the fact that his friends had so misled him, or for the fact that he had had such friends, made him even more retiring, and to this the death of his parents contributed.

On the other hand, the esteem in which he was held by the head of the house increased with his efficiency. He was a man much trusted, and they had already begun to think of giving him a share in the business when he fell ill and was sick unto death. At the moment when he was closest to it and was about to set foot upon "the solemn bridge of death" there suddenly awoke in him a remembrance, a remembrance of that incident which till then had not existed for him in any real sense. In his remembrance of it that occurrence assumed a definite form which brought his life to an end along with the loss of his purity. He recovered, but when he left his couch with health restored he took with him a *possibility*, and this possibility pursued him, and he pursued this possibility in his passionate investigation, and this possibility brooded in his silence, and this possibility it was that set in manifold motion the features of his face when he saw a child—and this possibility was that another being owed its life to him. And what he sought so anxiously, and what made him old when he was barely a man in years, was the unfortunate child, or the query whether there was such a child; and what made him a lunatic was the fact that every obvious way to discovery was cut off from him, inasmuch as the two who had been his destruction had long ago journeyed to America and disappeared; and what made his lunacy so dialectical was the fact that he did not so much as know whether his notion was a result of his illness, a fevered imagination, or whether death had actually come to the aid of his memory with a recollection of reality. Behold, it ended therefore with his wandering silently with bowed head along that short path between the hours of eleven and twelve, and with his wandering the rest of the day along the prodigious detour of the desperate windings of all possibilities, to find if possible a certainty, and then the thing to be sought.

However, in the beginning he was quite capable of attending to the business of the office. He was as precise and punctual as ever. He scanned the ledger and the letter-books, but now and then it came to him in a flash that the whole thing was labor lost, that there was something quite different he ought to be scanning; he closed the yearly statement of accounts, but in a flash this appeared to him a jest when he thought of his prodigious accountability.

Then the head of the firm died, leaving great wealth, and as he had loved the bookkeeper like a son, being himself without children, he made him heir to a fortune as if he had been a son. Thereupon the bookkeeper closed the account and became a man of science.

Now he had *otium*.[55] His anxious remembrance might not

perhaps have become a fixed idea if life had not inserted one of those casual circumstances which sometimes turn the scale. The only kinsman he had left was an old man, the cousin of his deceased mother, whom he called Cousin κατ᾽ ἐξοχήν.[56] This was an old bachelor to whom he betook himself after the death of his parents, and in whose house he dined every day, continuing this practice even after he had ceased to be in business. The cousin took delight in a certain sort of equivocal wit which (as psychology easily explains) is more often heard from old men than from the young. It is certain that when all hath been heard and most of it forgotten a simple open-hearted word in an old man's mouth may acquire a weight it otherwise does not have, it is also certain that an equivocal expression, a careless word, in the mouth of one stricken in years may easily have a disturbing effect, more especially when one is so much disposed to infection as the bookkeeper was. Among the recurrent witticisms to which the cousin repeatedly returned there was one standing joke, namely, that no man, not even a married man, could know definitely how many children he had. This was a way the cousin had, who for the rest was a good fellow, what one calls a boon companion, fond of a merry party, but the equivocal jest and his pinch of snuff he couldn't get along without. So there is no doubt that the bookkeeper had heard the cousin go through his whole repertoire a number of times, with that equivocal jest included, but without comprehending it or in any real sense hearing it. Now on the other hand it was aimed steadily at his sore spot and was calculated to wound him where he was weak and suffering. He would fall into one of his reveries, and when the cousin's jest should have given spice to the conversation it was the accidental touch which developed the elasticity of his fixed idea so that it established itself more and more securely. The silence of the reserved man and the wit of the loquacious cousin worked together upon the unfortunate until at last the understanding seriously resolved upon a change of masters because it could not endure serving with such housekeeping, and the bookkeeper exchanged understanding for lunacy.

113

In the capital there is traffic and tumult in the streets, at Christianshavn there prevails a quiet repose. There people do not seem to be acquainted with the aims and purposes which prompt the inhabitants of the metropolis to such noisy activity, do not seem to be acquainted with the diversities which underlie the clamorous movement of the capital. It was at Christianshavn the poor bookkeeper dwelt; there, in the practical sense of the word, he had his home, there, in the poetical sense, he was at home. But whether it was along the specialized historical path of investigation he sought to penetrate to the origin of that reminiscence, or whether it was by the prodigious detour of ordinary human observation that he sought wearily, with only the support of deceptive hypotheses, to transform that x into a known quantity—he did not find what he sought. It seemed to him sometimes that the object of his search might be very far off, sometimes that it was so near to him that he was sensible only of his own contrition when the poor thanked him on behalf of their children for his lavish gifts. It seemed to him as if he were dispensing himself from the performance of the most sacred duty, it seemed to him the most horrible thing that a father should give alms to his own child. Hence he would have no thanks, lest this gratitude might be a curse to him, but for all that he could not cease to give. And seldom have the poor found a benefactor so "generous and noble" and received help on such favorable terms.

An intelligent physician, viewing the case in a more general light, would of course have been able to remove from his mind this possibility which was the origin of all the rest; and even if, accommodating himself to the sick man's fancy in order to venture another method of cure, he had admitted this as a dolorous certainty, he still would have been able by his knowledge as a physician to remove the deduction from this certainty through a sequence of so many possibilities to so remote a distance that no one would be able to descry it . . . . . except the crazy man, who perhaps would only be the more deranged by such treatment. Such various effects has possibility. It is

114

used as a file: if the body is hard, the sharp edge can be filed off; but if it is soft in temper like a saw, the teeth of the saw only become sharper by filing. Every new possibility the poor bookkeeper discovered sharpened the saw of anxiety with which he was sawing alone and from the bite of which he himself was suffering.

I often saw him over there when he wandered along the waterfront, and I saw him also on other occasions; but once I encountered him in a coffee house of that neighborhood. I soon learned that every fourteenth day he came there in the evening. He read the papers, drank a glass of punch and talked with an old ship's captain who came there regularly every evening. The captain was well up in the seventies, white-haired, with a wholesome complexion and unimpaired health; his whole person showed no indication that except as a sailor he had been much tossed about in the world, and doubtless this impression was correct. How these two got to know one another I never learned, but it was a coffee house acquaintance, and they saw one another only in that place, where they talked with one another, now in English, now in Danish, now in a mixture of both. The bookkeeper was an entirely different man, he looked so roguish one could hardly recognize him as he entered the door with an English greeting which gave cheer to the old sailor. The captain's eyes were not of the best, with advancing years he had lost the capacity for judging people by their appearance. This explains how the bookkeeper, who was in his fortieth year and here looked much younger than he did elsewhere, could make the captain believe he was sixty years old and could maintain this fiction. In his youth the captain had been, as a sailor can be in all decency, a jolly good fellow, but doubtless in all decency, for he had such a worthy air and his whole nature was so lovable that one could vouch for his life and for his smartness as a sailor. He never tired of telling tales about dance-halls in London and larks with girls and then about India. Thereupon they drank to one another in the course of the conversation, and the captain said,

"Yes, that was in our youth, now we are old—but I should not say 'we,' for how old are you?" "Sixty," replied the book-keeper, and again they drank to one another.—Poor book-keeper, this was the only compensation for a lost youth, and even this compensation was the effect of contrast with the all too serious brooding of insanity. The whole situation was so humoristically planned, the deceit about the sixty years sup-ported by the use of the English language was so profoundly thought out with a view particularly to the humorous effect, that it impressed upon me how much one can learn from a lunatic.

Finally the bookkeeper died. He was ill several days, and when death came in earnest and he now was about to tread in earnest the dreadful bridge of eternity, the possibility van-ished, it had been nothing but a delirium; but his works did follow him, and with them the blessing of the poor, and there remained also in the souls of the children the remembrance of how much he had done for them. I followed him to the inter-ment. I chanced to be driving back from the grave along with the cousin. I knew that the bookkeeper had made a will and that the cousin was far from being covetous. I therefore took the liberty of saying that there was something very sad in the fact that he had no family of his own which could inherit what fortune he might leave, in the fact that he had not been mar-ried and left no children. Although the cousin was really affected by the death, more so than I could have expected, and on the whole produced a more favorable impression than I had foreboded, he could not refrain from saying, "Yes, my good friend, no man, not even the married man, can know definitely how many children he leaves behind him." To me the redeeming feature was that this was an adage, which per-haps he was hardly conscious of repeating, the pitiful thing was that he had such an adage. I have known criminals in prison who were really reformed, had really got an impression of something higher, and whose lives bore witness to it, yet to whom it would occur that in the midst of their serious talk about religion the most abominable reminiscences were mingled, and that in such a way that they were not aware of it at all.

Longbridge gets its name from its length, for as a bridge it is long, though as a road the length of the bridge is not very considerable, as one can convince oneself by crossing it. When one is standing on the other side, in Christianshavn, it seems as though after all the bridge must be very long, for it seems as though one were far, very far away from Copenhagen.

Quidam in *Stages on Life's Way*, pp. 258-68 (*SV* VIII 91-102)

118

The Wayfarer

*To what shall we compare the unchangeableness of God
amid our human longings?*

Imagine a wayfarer. He has been brought to a standstill at
the foot of a mountain, tremendous, impassable. It is this
mountain . . . . . no, it is not his destiny to cross it, but he
has set his heart upon the crossing; for his wishes, his longings, his desires, his very soul, which has an easier mode of
conveyance, are already on the other side; it only remains for
him to follow. Imagine him coming to be seventy years old;
but the mountain still stands there, unchanged, impassable. Let
him become twice seventy years; but the mountain stands
there unalterably blocking his way, unchanged, impassable.
Under all this he undergoes changes, perhaps; he dies away
from his longings, his wishes, his desires; he now scarcely
recognizes himself. And so a new generation finds him, altered, sitting at the foot of the mountain, which still stands
there, unchanged, impassable. Suppose it to have happened a
thousand years ago: the altered wayfarer is long since dead,
and only a legend keeps his memory alive; it is the only thing
that remains—aye, and also the mountain, unchanged, impassable. And now think of Him who is eternally unchange-
able, for whom a thousand years are but as one day—ah, even
this is too much to say, they are for Him as an instant, as if
they did not even exist. . . .

Anyone not eternally sure of Himself could not keep so still,
but would rise in His strength. Only one who is eternally im-
mutable can be in this manner so still.

He gives men time, and He can afford to give them time,
since He has eternity and is eternally unchanging.

Judge for Yourselves!, pp. 232-34 (*SV* XVII 259-61)

A Leper's Soliloquy

*When one suffers secretly and alone, yet freely for others,
what sort of existence relation emerges?*

[THE SCENE[57] IS AMONG THE GRAVES AT DAWN, SIMON LEPROSUS
IS SITTING ON A TOMBSTONE, HE HAS FALLEN ASLEEP, HE WAKES
AND CRIES OUT:]

SIMON!—"Yes."—Simon!—"Yes, who is calling?"—Where
art thou Simon?—"Here. With whom are you speaking?"—
With myself.—"Is it with yourself? How disgusting you are
with your corrupted flesh, a pestilence to every living thing,
avaunt from me, you abomination, betake yourself to the
tombs." Why am I the only one who cannot talk thus and act
accordingly? Everyone else, if I do not flee from him, flees
from me and leaves me alone. Does not an artist conceal himself in order to be a secret witness of how his work of art is
admired? Why cannot I separate that disgusting figure from
me and be secretly a witness of men's abhorrence? Why must
I be doomed to carry it about and show it off, as if I were a
vain artist who in his proper person must hear the admiration?
Why must I fill the desert with my cry and be company for the
wild beasts and abbreviate the time by my howling? This is
no exclamation, it is a question; I put the question to Him
who Himself has said that it is not good for a man to be without society. Is this my society? Is this the mate I am to seek—
the hungry monsters and the dead who have no fear of con-
tagion?

[HE SITS DOWN AGAIN, LOOKS ABOUT HIM AND SAYS TO HIMSELF:]

What has become of Manasseh? [lifting up his voice]
Manasseh!—[*He is silent a moment*]. So then he has wandered
off to the city. Yes, I know it. An ointment I have discovered,

by the use of which all leprosy turns inward so that none can see it and the priest must declare us whole. I taught him how to use it. I told him that the sickness did not therefore cease, that it became internal and that one's breath could infect another and make him visibly leprous. Then he was jubilant, he hates existence, he curses men, he would avenge himself, he runs to the city, he breathes poison upon all. Manasseh, Manasseh, why did you give place in your soul to the devil, was it not enough that your body was leprous?

I will cast away the remainder of the ointment so that I never may be tempted. Father Abraham's God, let me forget how it was prepared! Father Abraham, when I am dead I shall awaken in your bosom, then I shall eat with the purest, you indeed are not fearful of the leper. Isaac and Jacob, you are not afraid to sit at table with one who was a leper and was loathed by men. You dead who sleep here around me, awake, just for an instant, hear a word, only one word, great Abraham from me because he has a place among the blessed prepared for him who had no place among men.

What is human compassion after all! To whom is it rightly due unless to the unfortunate, and how is it paid to him? The impoverished man falls into the hands of the usurer, who at the last helps him into prison as a slave—so also do the fortunate practice usury and regard the unfortunate as a sacrifice, thinking that they purchase the friendship of God at a cheap price, yea, by unlawful means. A little gift, a mite, when they themselves possess abundance, a visit when it involves no danger, a bit of sympathy which by contrast may season their lavish living—behold, that is the sacrifice of compassion! But if there is danger, they chase the unfortunate out into the desert so as not to hear his cry which might disturb music and dancing and luxurious living, and might condemn compassion—human compassion, which would deceive God and the unfortunate.

So seek then in vain for compassion in the city and among the fortunate, seek it out here in the desert. I thank Thee, Thou God of Abraham, that Thou didst permit me to discover this ointment, I thank Thee that Thou didst sustain me in renouncing the use of it; I understand however Thy loving kindness in that I voluntarily endure my fate, freely suffering what necessity imposes. If no one has had compassion upon me, what wonder that compassion has fled like me out among the graves, where I sit comforted as one who sacrifices his life to save others, as one who voluntarily chooses banishment to save others. Thou God of Abraham, give them corn and new wine in abundance and prosperous seasons, build the barns greater and give abundance greater than the barns, give to the fathers wisdom, to the mothers fruitfulness, and to the children a blessing, give victory in battle, that it may be the people of Thy possession. Hear the prayer of him whose body is infected and impure, a horror to the people, to the happy ones a snare, hear him if for all that his heart was not tainted.

Simon leprosus was a Jew. If he had lived in Christendom, he would have found a very different sort of sympathy. Whenever in the course of the year the sermon is about the ten lepers, the priest protests that he too has felt as if he were a leper—but when there is typhus. . . . .

Quidam in *Stages on Life's Way*, pp. 220-22 (*SV* VIII 51-54)

The Dangerous Instrument

Is love, in the Christian sense, dangerous?

I wonder if a man handing another man an extremely sharp, polished, two-edged instrument would hand it over with the air, gestures, and expression of one delivering a bouquet of flowers? Would not this be madness? What does one do, then? Convinced of the excellence of the dangerous instrument, one recommends it unreservedly, to be sure, but in such a way that in a certain sense one warns against it. So it is with Christianity. If what is needed is to be done, we should not hesitate, aware of *the highest responsibility*, to preach *in Christian sermons*—yes, precisely *in Christian sermons*—AGAINST Christianity.

Works of Love, p. 191 *(SV* XII 191)

The Jeweller

*To what shall we compare the jumble of foolishness
and wisdom of young love?*

Imagine a jeweller who had developed to such an extent his
knowledge of precious stones that his whole life was in this
distinction between genuine and false, suppose he saw a child
playing with a variety of stones, genuine and false, mingled
together, and having equal delight in both—I think he would
shudder inwardly at seeing the absolute distinction resolved;
but in case he beheld the child's happiness, its delight in the
game, he perhaps would humble himself under it and be absorbed in this "shuddering" sight.

Quidam in *Stages on Life's Way*, p. 205 (*SV* VIII 37)

The Amusement of the Gods

Of all wishes, which is best?

Something wonderful has happened to me. I was caught up into the seventh heaven. There sat all the gods in assembly. By special grace I was granted the privilege of making a wish. "Wilt thou," said Mercury, "Have youth or beauty or power or a long life or the most beautiful maiden or any of the other glories we have in the chest? Choose, but only one thing." For a moment I was at a loss. Then I addressed myself to the gods as follows: "Most honorable contemporaries, I choose this one thing, that I may always have the laugh on my side." Not one of the gods said a word; on the contrary, they all began to laugh. From that I concluded that my wish was granted, and found that the gods knew how to express themselves with taste; for it would hardly have been suitable for them to have answered gravely: "Thy wish is granted."

"A" in *Either/Or*, I, pp. 41-42 (*SV* II 44)

125

The Wife of the Orientalist

What is the difference between marriage as an ethical relation and courtship as an aesthetic relation?

Somewhere in Holland there lived a learned man, he was an orientalist and was married. One day he did not come to the midday meal, although he was called. His wife waits longingly, looking at the food, and the longer this lasts the less she can explain his failure to appear. Finally she resolves to go over to his room and exhort him to come. There he sits alone in his work-room, there is nobody with him. He is absorbed in his oriental studies. I can picture it to myself. She has bent over him, laid her arm about his shoulders, peered down at the book, thereupon looked at him and said, "Dear friend, why do you not come over to eat?" The learned man perhaps has hardly had time to take account of what was said, but looking at his wife he presumably replied, "Well, my girl, there can be no question of dinner, here is a vocalization I have never seen before. I have often seen the passage quoted, but never like this, and yet my edition is an excellent Dutch edition. Look at this dot here! It is enough to drive one mad." I can imagine that his wife looked at him, half-smiling, half-deprecating that such a little dot should disturb the domestic order, and the report recounts that she replied, "Is that anything to take so much to heart? It is not worth wasting one's breath on it." No sooner said than done. She blows, and behold the vocalization disappears, for this remarkable dot was a grain of snuff. Joyfully the scholar hastens to the dinner table, joyful at the fact that the vocalization had disappeared, still more joyful in his wife.

Do I need to draw out the moral from this story? If that scholar had not been married, he perhaps would have gone crazy, perhaps he would have taken several orientalists with him, for I doubt not that he would have raised a terrible alarm in the literary organs. . . . If that scholar had not been married, if he had been an aestheticist who had in his power all the requisites, perhaps then he would have become the lucky man to whom that marvelous maiden wished to belong. He would not have married, their sentiments were too superior for that. He would have built her a palace and would have spared no refinement to make her life rich in enjoyment, he would have visited her in her castle, for so she wished it to be; with erotic coquetry he would have made his way to her on foot while his valets followed him in a carriage, bringing rich and costly gifts. So, then, in the course of his oriental studies he stumbled upon that remarkable vocalization. He would have stared at it without being able to explain it. The moment, however, was come when he should make his visit to the ladylove. He would have cast this care aside, for how could he becomingly make a visit to a ladylove with thoughts of anything else but of her charms and of his own love? He would have assumed an air of the utmost amiability, he would have been more fascinating than ever, and would have pleased her beyond all measure because in his voice there was a distant resonance of many passions, because out of despondency he had to contend for cheerfulness. But when at dawn he left her, when he had thrown her the last kiss and then sat in his carriage, his brow was darkened. He arrived home, the shutters were closed in his study, the lamps lit, he would not be undressed but sat and stared at the dot he could not explain. He had indeed a girl whom he loved, yea, perhaps adored, but he visited her only when his soul was rich and strong, but he had no helpmeet who came in and called him at midday, no wife who could blow the dot away.

Judge William in *Either/Or*, II, pp. 313-15 (*SV* III 284-85)

The Needlewoman

How should one listen to an edifying discourse?

When a woman makes an altar cloth, so far as she is able, she makes every flower as lovely as the graceful flowers of the field, as far as she is able, every star as sparkling as the glistening stars of the night. She withholds nothing, but uses the most precious things she possesses. She sells off every other claim upon her life that she may purchase the most uninterrupted and favorable time of the day and night for her one and only, for her beloved work. But when the cloth is finished and put to its sacred use: then she is deeply distressed if someone should make the mistake of looking at her art, instead of the meaning of the cloth; or make the mistake of looking at a defect, instead of at the meaning of the cloth. For she could not work the sacred meaning into the cloth itself, nor could she sew it on the cloth as though it were one more ornament.

Purity of Heart, pp. 27-28 (*SV* XI 13-14)

The Royal Theater

How may individual conscience be distinguished from an overarching perspective on world history as a whole?

A king sometimes has a royal theater reserved for himself, but the difference which here excludes the ordinary citizen is accidental. It is otherwise when we speak of God and the royal theater He has for Himself. The ethical development of the individual constitutes the little private theater where God is indeed a spectator, but where the individual is also a spectator from time to time, although essentially he is an actor, whose task is not to deceive but to reveal, just as all ethical development consists in becoming apparent before God. But world-history is the royal stage where God is spectator, where He is not accidentally but essentially the only spectator, because He is the only one who *can* be.

Johannes Climacus in *Concluding Unscientific Postscript*,
p. 141 (*SV* IX 131)

The Professor's Defense

Does expression gain by repetition?

When in his time Professor Ussing made an address before the 28th of May Association and something in it met with disapprobation, what then did the professor do? Being at that period always resolute and *gewaltig*,[58] he pounded on the table and said, "I repeat it." So on that occasion his opinion was that what he had said gained by repetition. A few years ago I heard a parson deliver on two successive Sundays exactly the same discourse. If he had been of the opinion of the professor as he ascended the pulpit on the second occasion he would have pounded the desk and said, "I repeat what I said last Sunday."

Constantine Constantius in *Repetition*, p. 53 (*SV* V 141)

Notes

1. Phalaris, tyrant of Agrigento in Sicily, ca. 570-554 B.C., see Lucian of Samosata, *Lucian*, Vol. I., pp. 1-31; cf. *TC*, p. 248. This parable is the first paragraph of the "Diapsalmata" (refrains) that begin Kierkegaard's first pseudonymous work, *E/O*.

2. Climacus is comparing his *Philosophical Fragments* to the idle activity of Diogenes; cf. *Lucian*, Vol. VI, p. 5.

3. Louis Adolphe Thiers, 1797-1877, twice premier under Louis Philippe.

4. For another version of this same premise, see *JP* II 266 (V A 85).

5. Peder Tordenskjold, 1691-1720, was a Norwegian-Danish folk hero who deceived the Swedish (*JP* IV, 137f). A year after the events of a disruptive love affair, Quidam, one of Kierkegaard's most dialectically introspective pseudonyms, is found in his Diary to be reflecting constantly on the meaning of those interpersonal traumas, which pass by like an endless parade in his unsettled mind.

6. Omission in English translation.

7. "Fra det Øieblik" omitted in English translation.

8. This parable appears in "the rotation method," where Kierkegaard caricatures, through his aesthetic pseudonym "A," the outcome of a constricted aestheticism that despairingly searches for immediate pleasure without ethical reference.

9. In his Journal of 1849, Kierkegaard sketched the same theme in this way: "What would one think of a district judge who read an order from his chief not as an order but as a literary production, evaluating it and examining it critically, under the impression that this was his task, and then even submitted his well-written critique to the chief" (*JP* III 29 [X^1 A 465]).

10. *The Ethics of Aristotle*, Book Three, ch. v, p. 75.

11. Revision of English translation.

12. The legend of Parmeniscus, a Pythagorean, was related by Athenaeus, *The Deipnosophists*, tr. C. B. Gulick (London: W. Heinemann, 1950), 7 vols., Vol. VI, Book Fourteen, section 614, pp. 306f.

13. Franz Theremin, 1780-1846, German pastor, preacher to the court and professor of theology in the University of Berlin.

14. "The blood of the martyrs is the seed of the church." Adapted from Tertullian, *Apology, De Spectaculus*, tr. T. R. Glover [with Minucius Felix, *Octavius*, tr. G. H. Randall] (London: W. Heinemann, 1931), p. 227.

15. This parable appears in the last chapter of *PF*, where Climacus is considering the difficulties experienced by "the disciple at second hand" (as distinguished from the first generation of immediate witnesses to the redemptive event) who may try to secure faith by means of historical inquiry. The immediate context of the parable is this: Suppose one is analyzing the historical knowledge of subsequent generations of disciples. Although one might think that the earlier generation enjoys "the (relative) advantage of being nearer to an immediate certainty," this parable shows that to be an "illusory advantage: for he who is not so near to immediate certainty as to be immediately certain is absolutely separated from it" (*PF*, p. 114).

16. According to legend, Ptolemy of Egypt secured the Greek translation of the Old Testament by locking up the seventy-two translators for seventy-two days until each had translated the entire Old Testament, whereupon it was discovered that all the translations miraculously were the same.

17. For an explanation of "The God," see *PF*, pp. ix-xi.

18. This parable is not a polemic against historical inquiry, but against the illusory assumption that objective historical investigation can elicit faith.

19. Lowrie's text corrects Kierkegaard's, which read "East."

20. For the biblical account of Solomon's succession of David, see I Kings 1-11.

21. God's communication with humanity is indirect in the sense that it confronts the hearer with a fundamental decision about her/himself. By analogy, instead of asking for verbal reassurances of love, the lover in the parable asks for a decision of the beloved.

22. This parable is the last paragraph of *FT*, which by implication points beyond itself to a subsequent clarification of religious existence that would come later in *TC* and the *CD*. Cf. W. G. Tennemann, I, p. 220.

23. Danish "en ringe Pige" means a maiden of the poorest and most deprived class. This parable of the means by which God

overcomes the distance between God and humanity is the center-piece of *PF* and the most condensed way of capturing that book's essential argument. No parable of this collection is more important or influential, and none better reveals the central intent of Kierkegaard's authorship.

24. Callicles, not Polos, as Climacus suggests. Cf. Plato, "Gorgias," section 45, pp. 158-59.

25. Plutarch *Lives*, Vol. 2, p. 79.

26. The context in which this parable occurs is immediately following "A Project of Thought," *PF*, ch. 1, which asks whether it is possible to base an eternal happiness on a point of departure in time? If the moment in time (an unimportant occasion for Socratic *anamnesis*) should come to have decisive significance for learning the truth, what would be the consequences? If one supposes that the eternal comes into being in the moment, then the antecedent state of the learner is error and the teacher is God himself, who acting as an occasion prompts the learner to recall that he is in error, restores the lost condition for understanding the truth and gives the learner the truth. Such a teacher one would never be able to forget, and such a moment would be called "the fullness of time." This is the essence of "A Project of Thought," which then moves in ch. 2 to this affirmation: "Moved by love, the God is thus eternally resolved to reveal himself." This is followed by "The King and the Maiden," which presents a parabolic answer to the essential dilemma: "the difference between them." It may seem a small matter for the God to overcome this difference, but it cannot be done authentically by "annihilating the unlikeness." The God's revelation of his love is made more difficult and more unhappy in its prospect because the means of revealing his love must correspond with its end. For it is only in equality that an understanding can be effected. This is the problem to which the parable speaks, which Climacus warns us (p. 31) not to be too quick to "solve" in a premature way.

27. "Kierkegaard consciously writes 'Platonically' here," notes Niels Thulstrup (*PF*, p. 190n), "and therefore does not say 'by God' but 'by the God.'" For a discussion of why Kierkegaard uses the unusual expression *Guden* ("the God") rather than *Gud* (God), see *PF*, pp. ix-xii. The reader will note that there are a number of omissions in this edition's rendering of the parable, and the original text should be consulted for the full rendering. Portions omitted are brief excursi and temporary diversions from

the parable itself. Furthermore, the three paragraphs beginning "Moved by Love" have been shifted out of their original position in order to *begin* the parable at its obvious beginning point ("Suppose there was a king. . .") without having to omit the content of these three crucial paragraphs.

28. Matthew 9:23.

29. Contra Docetism which denies Christ's true humanity.

30. Plato, "Symposium," section 220, pp. 272-73.

31. Matthew 27:46.

32. John 19:5.

33. Vigilius Haufniensis in the *COD*, p. 61.

34. Thus, one may, precisely by repeating that which is generally accepted as the objective truth, prove himself to be not yet sane, although the cure does not consist in rejecting objective truth either. "The objective truth as such, is by no means adequate to determine that whoever utters it is sane; on the contrary, it may even betray the fact that he is mad, although what he says may be entirely true, and especially objectively true" (*CUP*, p. 174).

35. Cf. I Corinthians 2:9.

36. Overmuch.

37. In his Journal (V A 45), Kierkegaard indicates that he had been reading the French mystical theologian, François Fénelon (1651-1715). See Fénelon's *Lives of the Ancient Philosophers* (New York, 1841).

38. "Periander" shows that Kierkegaard had intuited the essential dynamics of the Oedipal complex many decades before Freud. For Periander, like Oedipus, destroys others and finally himself out of an overweening sense of guilt and shame that arose in part from his incestuous relationship with his mother.

39. Quoting Diogenes Laertii, *De Vitis philosophorum* (Leipzig: Sumptibus Ottonis Holtze, 1884), Lib. I, Cap. VII, pp. 45-48.

40. Is Quidam himself like Periander? So it seems from his previous entry of April 18, *SLW*, p. 586, when he speaks of himself as feeling very stupid amid all his shrewdness. Lowrie's speculation, however (*SLW*, p. 298n), that "it is his father we must discover in Periander, while he is the exiled son, and the brother is Peter Kierkegaard," is far-fetched.

41. A motto on the shield of Baron Andre Taifel, as reported in Gottfried Wilhelm Liebniz, *Opera Philosophica*, ed. J. E. Erdmann (Berlin, 1839-40), p. 652.

42. This parable, which Kierkegaard entitles "A School Exer-

cise: Periander," is a seemingly endless sequence of tragic decisions that express a continuing moral dialectic in their inexorable strain of consequences. Having taught classical languages in the Borgerdydskole in Copenhagen, Kierkegaard may have taken his young students through precisely this exercise in moral reflection.

43. In his Journal of 1854-55 Kierkegaard used the same image with a different effect. See *JP* III 59 (XI² A 390), and *AC*.

44. The same pseudonym appears in the last segment of *E/O*, Vol. I, "Diary of the Seducer," pp. 249-371. Lest one imagine that this is Kierkegaard's last word on woman, it should be remembered that other pseudonyms, especially Judge William, vigorously attack Johannes' views as a misguided and dehumanized conception of woman. For, according to Judge William (*E/O* II and *SLW*, pp 94ff), Johannes fails to understand the moral dimension of sexuality, and the promise of combining erotic love and faithful commitment in an enduring choice (marriage).

45. "The task of becoming subjective, then, may be presumed to be the highest task, and one that is proposed to every human being. . . . Furthermore . . . the task of becoming subjective furnishes a human being with enough to do to suffice him for his entire life" (*CUP*, p. 146).

46. All three characters in the parable are standing before a mirror in which each sees a melancholy vision of himself reflected: Swift sees the "poor old man"; the father, looking in the son's face, recognizes his son's quiet despair and in that his own guilt; the son, looking in the mirror of his father's face, experiences in his father's sorrow a curious sense of edification. Quidam reveals through this parable the character of many subtle human interactions that involve unclarified guilt and responsibility for a significant other whose level of understanding is never fully revealed, and yet the gaze is remembered poignantly. In such interactions one experiences this double mirror effect, where each face mirrors the other's care, responsibility, and pathos toward the beholder. Such a memory may survive the death of the partner, as Kierkegaard's memory of his father's awareness of his melancholy remained a real presence to him long after his father's death.

47. Omission in English translation.

48. Enemas.

49. "Nebuchadnezzar" is among the most unusual of all of Kierkegaard's parables, distinct in its use of the premise that it is written as if it were scripture, with fantasized verse numbers and

language saturated with biblical imagery. In fact this parable grows directly out of Daniel 4 and is best interpreted in close correlation with it. Chaldean king Nebuchadnezzar (d. 562 B.C.), living amid luxury, had a dream that terrified him, of a great tree at the center of the earth reaching to the sky under which wild beasts found shelter, and a second dream of a tree hewn down to a stump on which was tethered a beast. After all the king's diviners failed to explain them, the young exiled Jew Daniel interpreted the dreams as a prophecy that Nebuchadnezzar, whose power was a divine gift, would be banished from the society of mankind and would live as a beast, feeding on grass. All this came to pass, according to Daniel 4, at the end of which time Nebuchadnezzar was restored to his throne, glorifying God. It is this pattern of transmutation and return that Quidam develops on the premise that this parable is a subjective report of the changing consciousness of Nebuchadnezzar. This is the sixth and last of the major parables of Quidam's Diary, all of them date the fifth of the month at midnight (an indication of their autobiographical character according to Lowrie, since Kierkegaard was born on the fifth day of the fifth month). The others are "The Quiet Despair," "The Leper's Soliloquy," "Solomon's Dream," "A Possibility," and "Periander." Lowrie views "Nebuchadnezzar" as "a fantastic description of S. K.'s religious conversion, which he persisted in ascribing to his experience with Regina" (*SLW*, p. 330n).

50. Vocation. Cf. Horace, *Odes and Epodes*, tr. Paul Shorey (New York: Benjamin J. Sanborn & Co., 1919), Book I, Ode xxxii, p. 227.

51. In his Journal of 1843 Kierkegaard sketched the essential outline of this parable; see *JP* V 241 (IV A 147).

52. A figure in a story by Ernst Theodor Amadeus Hoffmann, *Ausgewahlte Schriften*, 15 vols., ed. E. Grisebach, 1899, "*Die Königsbraut.*"

53. Cf. *SLW*, "In Vino Veritas."

54. For an interpretation of this parable as an autobiographical portrayal of SK's "sexual fall" in May 1836, see Lowrie, *Kierkegaard*, pp. 132ff.

55. Leisure time.

56. In special degree, or "special cousin."

57. One of the most penetrating and important of Kierkegaard's parables, and quite different from all the others (since it is written in the form of a soliloquy), "The Leper's Soliloquy" requires some

unpacking. Painstakingly constructed and economically executed, the parable is clearly divided in three sequential parts that traverse the aesthetic, ethical, and religious modes of consciousness in the persona of Simon the leper.

In the first paragraph the complaint expresses the stage of aesthetic immediacy, of Simon's experiencing of himself as alienated, despairing over his limitation. In the second paragraph we learn the ethical dilemma implicit in his discovery of the ointment. The choice is clear: the way out is individually liberating, but socially disastrous. The remainder of the parable expresses Simon's choice and his reflection on it, which is rooted in a religious perspective on his suffering.

The final paragraph is an ironic addendum in which the situation of Simon leprosus, the Jew, is contrasted with the hypocritical situation of civil religion in Christendom. Since Christendom speaks a great deal of redemptive suffering, one might expect it to be wholly sympathetic with the leper, but in Christendom an ironic form of "sympathy" is found: sermons about sacrifice, but avoidance of the typhus epidemic.

58. Powerful, vehement.

Bibliography

Kierkegaard's Works in Chronological Order

The Concept of Irony, tr. Lee Capel, New York: Harper and Row, 1966. (*Om Begrebet Ironi*, 1841.)

Either/Or, I, tr. David F. Swenson and Lillian Marvin Swenson; II, tr. Walter Lowrie; 2 ed. rev. Howard A. Johnson, Princeton: Princeton University Press, 1971. (*Enten-Eller*, I-II, 1843.)

Johannes Climacus or De omnibus dubitandum est, and A Sermon, tr. T. H. Croxall, London: Adam and Charles Black, 1958. (*Johannes Climacus eller De omnibus dubitandum est,** 1842-43.)

Edifying Discourses, I-IV, tr. David F. Swenson and Lillian Marvin Swenson, Minneapolis: Augsburg Publishing House, 1943-46. (*Opbyggelige Taler*, 1843-44.)

Fear and Trembling (with *The Sickness unto Death*), tr. Walter Lowrie, Princeton: Princeton University Press, 1968. (*Frygt og Bæven*, 1843.)

Repetition, tr. Walter Lowrie, Princeton: Princeton University Press, 1941. (*Gientagelsen*, 1843.)

Philosophical Fragments, tr. David Swenson, 2 ed. rev. Howard Hong, Princeton: Princeton University Press, 1962. (*Philosophiske Smuler*, 1844.)

The Concept of Dread, tr. Walter Lowrie, 2 ed., Princeton: Princeton University Press, 1957. (*Begrebet Angest*, 1844.)

Thoughts on Crucial Situations in Human Life, tr. David F. Swenson, ed. Lillian Marvin Swenson, Minneapolis: Augsburg Publishing House, 1941. (*Tre Taler ved tænkte Leiligheder*, 1845.)

Stages on Life's Way, tr. Walter Lowrie, Princeton: Princeton University Press, 1940. (*Stadier paa Livets Vej*, 1845.)

* Published posthumously.

Concluding Unscientific Postscript, tr. David F. Swenson and Walter Lowrie, Princeton: Princeton University Press for American Scandinavian Foundation, 1941. (*Afsluttende uvidenskabelig Efterskrift*, 1846.)

The Present Age and *Of the Difference Between A Genius and An Apostle*, tr. Alexander Dru, New York: Harper and Row, 1962. (*En literair Anmeldelse, To Tidsaldre*, 1846.)

On Authority and Revelation, The Book on Adler, tr. Walter Lowrie, Princeton: Princeton University Press, 1955. (*Bogen om Adler*,* *Papirer VII*² B 235, 1846-47.)

Purity of Heart, tr. Douglas Steere, New York: Harper and Row, 1938. (*Opbyggelige Taler i forskjellig Aand*, Pt. 1, 1847.)

The Gospel of Suffering and The Lilies of the Field, tr. David F. Swenson and Lillian Marvin Swenson, Minneapolis: Augsburg Publishing House, 1948. (*Opbyggelige Taler i forskjellig Aand*, Pt. 2, 1847.)

Works of Love, tr. Howard and Edna Hong, New York: Harper and Row, 1962. (*Kjerlighedens Gjerninger*, 1847.)

Crisis in the Life of an Actress, tr. Stephen Crites, New York: Harper and Row, 1967. (*Krisen og en Krise i en Skuespillerindes Liv*, 1848.)

Christian Discourses, including The Lily of the Field and the Bird of the Air and Three Discourses at the Communion on Fridays, tr. Walter Lowrie, London and New York: Oxford University Press, 1940. (*Christelige Taler*, 1848. *Lilien paa Marken og Fuglen under Himlen*, 1849. *Tre Taler ved Altergangen om Fredagen*, 1849.)

The Sickness unto Death (with *Fear and Trembling*), tr. Walter Lowrie, Princeton: Princeton University Press, 1968. (*Sygdommen til Døden*, 1849.)

Training in Christianity, including "The Woman Who was a Sinner," tr. Walter Lowrie, Princeton: Princeton University Press, 1944. (*Indøvelse i Christendom*, 1850. *En opbyggelig Tale*, 1850.)

The Point of View for My Work as an Author, and *On My Work as an Author*, tr. Walter Lowrie, London: Oxford University Press, 1939. (*Synspunktet for min Forfatter-Virksomhed*,* 1859. *Om min Forfatter-Virksomhed*, 1851.)

For Self-Examination, and *Judge for Yourselves!* and *Three Discourses*, tr. Walter Lowrie, Princeton: Princeton University Press, 1944. (*Til Selvprøvelse*, 1851. *Dommer Selv!*, 1852. *To Taler ved Altergangen om Fredagen*, 1851.)

Attack Upon "Christendom," tr. Walter Lowrie, Princeton: Princeton University Press, 1944. (*Bladartikler*, 1854-55. *Øieblikket*, 1855. *Hvad Christus dømmer om officiel Christendom*, 1855.)

Søren Kierkegaard's Journals and Papers, tr. Howard V. Hong and Edna H. Hong, assisted by Gregor Malantschuk, Bloomington and London: Indiana University Press, I, 1967; II, 1970; III-IV, 1975; V, 1978; VI forthcoming. References cite volume and page number, with *Papirer** reference in parentheses.

General Bibliography

Aarne, Antti. *Types of the Folk Tale, A Classification and Bibliography*. New York: B. Franklin, 1971.

Aristotle. *The Ethics of Aristotle*, tr. J.A.K. Thompson. London: Allen and Unwin, 1953.

Auerbach, Erich. *Mimesis*. Princeton: Princeton University Press, 1953.

Barthes, Roland. *Critical Essays*, tr. R. Howard. Evanston: Northwestern University Press, 1972.

Blackman, E. C. "New Methods of Parable Interpretation," *Canadian Journal of Theology*, 15, 1969, 3-13.

Brandt, Frithiof. *Søren Kierkegaard*. Copenhagen: The Danish Society, 1963.

Cadoux, A. T. *The Parables of Jesus*. London: James Clarke, 1930.

Collins, James. *The Mind of Kierkegaard*. Chicago: Henry Regnery, 1953.

Crossan, John. *In Parables*. New York: Harper and Row, 1973.

Croxall, T. H. *Kierkegaard Commentary*. New York: Harper and Row, 1956.

Diem, Hermann. *Kierkegaard: An Introduction*, tr. David Green. Richmond: John Knox Press, 1966.

Dithmar, Reinhard. *Die Fabel: Geschichte, Struktur, Didaktik*. Paderborn: Ferdinand Schöningh, 1971.

Dodd. C. H. *The Parables of the Kingdom*. London: Collins, 1961.

Dupré, Louis. *Kierkegaard as Theologian*. New York: Sheed and Ward, 1963.

Eller, Vernard. *Kierkegaard and Radical Discipleship*. Princeton: Princeton University Press, 1968.

Elliott, R. C. *The Power of Satire*. Princeton: Princeton University Press, 1960.

Feldman, Asher. *Parables and Similies of the Rabbis.* Cambridge: Cambridge University Press, 1960.

Fry, Northrup. *Anatomy of Criticism.* Princeton: Princeton University Press, 1957.

Gide, André. *Two Legends: Oedipus and Theseus.* New York: Random House, 1958.

Grimm, Jakob and Wilhelm. *German Folk Tales.* Carbondale: Southern Illinois University Press, 1960.

Guillen, Claudio. *Literature as System: Essays Toward a Theory of Literary History.* Princeton: Princeton University Press, 1971.

Halevi, J. L. "Kierkegaard and the Midrash," *Judaism,* 4, 1955, 13-28.

Henriksen, Aage. "Kierkegaard's Reviews of Literature," *Orbis Litterarum,* 10, 1955, 75-83.

Hirsch, Emanuel. *Kierkegaard-Studien,* 2 vols. Gütersloh: C. Bertelsmann, 1930-33.

Hohlenberg, Johannes. *Søren Kierkegaard,* tr. T. H. Croxall. New York: Pantheon, 1954.

Honig, Edwin. *Dark Conceit.* London: Faber and Faber, 1959.

Jeremias, Joachim. *The Parables of Jesus.* New York: Charles Scribner's Sons, 1963.

Johnson, Howard, and Thulstrup, Niels, editors. *A Kierkegaard Critique.* New York: Harper and Row, 1962.

Jolivet, Regis. *Introduction to Kierkegaard.* New York: Dutton, 1951.

Jones, G. V. *The Art and Truth of the Parables.* London: S.P.C.K., 1964.

Jülicher, Adolf. *Die Gleichnisreden Jesu,* 2 vols. Tübingen: J.C.B. Mohr, 1899.

Kafka, Franz. *Parables and Paradoxes: Parabeln und Paradoxe.* New York: Schocken Books, 1961.

Kingsbury, J. D. "Major Trends in Parables Interpretation," *Concordia Theological Monthly,* 42, 1971, 579-96.

Lowrie, Walter. *Kierkegaard.* Oxford: Oxford University Press, 1938.

Lucian of Samosata, *Lucian*, 8 vols. London: William Heinemann, 1921 ff.

Mackey, Louis. *Kierkegaard: A Kind of Poet*. Philadelphia: University of Pennsylvania Press, 1971.

McKinnon, Alastair, *The Kierkegaard Indices*, 4 vols. Leiden: Brill, 1970-75.

McNiece, Louis. *Varieties of Parable*. Cambridge: Cambridge University Press, 1965.

Malantschuk, Gregor. *Kierkegaard's Thought*. Princeton: Princeton University Press, 1971.

Niedermeyer, Gerhard. *Søren Kierkegaard und die Romantik*. Leipzig: Quelle and Meyer, 1910.

Noel, Thomas. *Theories of the Fable in the Eighteenth Century*. New York: Columbia University Press, 1975.

Perrin, Norman. "The Parables of Jesus as Parables, as Metaphors, and as Aesthetic Objects: A Review Article," *Journal of Religion*, 47, 1967, 340-47.

Pivgevig, Edo. *Ironie als Daseinsform bei Søren Kierkegaard*. Gutersloh: Gutersloher, 1960.

Plato. *Phaedrus, Ion, Gorgias and Symposium*, tr. Lane Cooper. London: Oxford University Press, 1938.

Plutarch. *Lives*, tr. B. Perrin. Cambridge, Mass.: Harvard University Press, 1959.

Propp, Vladimir. *Morphology of the Folktale*. Austin: University of Texas Press, 1970.

Rohde, Peter. *Søren Kierkegaard*. London: George Allen and Unwin, 1963.

Scholes, Robert. *Structuralism in Literature*. New Haven: Yale University Press, 1976.

Shmuëli, Adi. *Kierkegaard and Consciousness*. Princeton: Princeton University Press, 1971.

Taylor, Mark C. *Kierkegaard's Pseudonymous Authorship*. Princeton: Princeton University Press, 1975.

Tennemann, W. G. *Geschichte der Philosophie*. Leipzig: Johann Ambrosius Barth, 1798.

Teselle, Sallie. *Speaking in Parables*. Philadelphia: Fortress Press. 1975.

Thompson, Josiah. *Kierkegaard*. New York: Knopf, 1973.

Via, Dan O., Jr. *The Parables: Their Literary and Existential Dimension*. Philadelphia: Fortress Press, 1967.

Wahl, Jean. *Kierkegaard et le romantisme*. Copenhagen: Symposion Kierkegaardianum, 1955.

Wheelwright, Philip. *The Burning Fountain*. Bloomington, Ind.: Indiana University Press, 1954.

Appendix

Supplementary List of Kierkegaard's Parables

What follows is not to be understood as an exhaustive inventory of all Kierkegaard's narratives that are potentially classifiable as parables, but a critical selection of his parables and stories that demonstrates the range and pervasiveness of parabolic communication throughout his entire literary effort. All Danish references, unless otherwise noted, are to the *Samlede Værker*, 3rd edition, edited by A. B. Drachmann, J. L. Heiberg and H. O. Lange, revised by Peter P. Rohde, 20 volumes (Copenhagen: Gyldendal, 1962-64).

Parable	Themes	Page (and line) Numbers	Danish Text
THE CONCEPT OF IRONY			
(*Om Begrebet Ironi, 1841*)			
The Grave of Napoleon	viewpoint, nothingness, Xenophon	56(19)-57(9)	I 78
Socrates in the Underworld	examination, wisdom, ignorance	75(1)-77(8)	I 93-96
The Sparkle of the Wine	eros, infinite, refraction	79(7-17)	I 97
The Currency of the Ironist	nothingness, concealment, health	88(29)-89(7)	I 106
The Convincing Dispute	irony, negation, habit, conversion	93(14-17)	I 110
The Password	unity, virtue, abstract	95(6-17)	I 112

147

Parable	Themes	Page (and line) Numbers	Danish Text
The Huckster and the Artist	irony, ideal, empirical, finitude	156(33)-158(23)	I 166-68
The Suspended Basket	ideality, Socrates, irony, comedy	180(10-37)	I 187-88
The Anger of the Gods	mission, irony, ignorance, emptiness	198(15)-199(10)	I 204
The Englishman Who Required an Unusual View	removal, prospect, enchantment	215(8-23)	I 219
The Fitting Punishment	congruity, state, guilt, vindication, comedy, irony, death	218(19)-221(13)	I 222-24
The Guadalquivir River	renewal, world history, uniqueness	222(1-17)	I 226
Dispatching the Ship of Speculation	infinite, beginning, discovery	239(8)-240(1)	I 241
The Shallow Barque of Charon	reality, ideality, negativity	255(12-21)	I 255-56
Intellectual Freemasonry	irony, the age, speeches, isolation	263(1)-264(7)	I 262-63
The Incognito Traveler	irony, indirect communication	265(21-34)	I 264-65
Raising the Bid	enthusiasm, ironic satisfaction, manipulation, humor	266(31)-267(34)	I 266
The Proposal	affair, social prerogative, deception	268(15-36)	I 267
The Crowing Rooster	paternity, confidants, authors	269(4-22)	I 268
The Arrested Chancellor	dissemblance, irony, mystification	269(29)-270(6)	I 268-69
The Man Who Searched For His Spectacles	philosophy, inadvertence	289(21-23)	I 285
Hercules and Antaeus	irony, hellenism, middle ages, myth, history	294(7)-295(9)	I 289-90
The Cock	poetic freedom, masquerade, possibility	298(35)-299(31)	I 293-94
The Beneficent Arrest	boredom, irony, continuity, unity	302(8-21)	I 296-97

148

Parable	Themes	Page (and line) Numbers	Danish Text
EITHER/OR, I-II			
(Enten-Eller, I, by "A"; II, by Judge William, 1843)			
VOLUME I			
The Death of Insects	joy, pleasure, death	20(5-7)	II 24
The Whipped Horses	stillness, suffering, weariness	21(17-22)	II 25
The Immobilized Chessman	immobility, game	21(26-28)	II 25
The Man with the Yellowish Green Coat	alienation, pathos, color	22(31)-23(12)	II 26
The Falling Spider	emptiness, future, insecurity	24(4-11)	II 27
The Whipped Top	doubt, falling	24(19-21)	II 28
Virgil the Magician	anticipation, temptation, caldron	26(22-30)	II 30
The Artist Pair	pathos, beauty, blindness, Mozart	29(21)-30(11)	II 32-33
The Sign in the Window	philosophy, disappointment, deception	31(25-29)	II 34
The Fenris Wolf	bondage, anxiety	33(28-37)	II 36
The Essay on Immortality	disenchantment, promise, doubt	34(1-26)	II 36-37
The Lüneburger Pig	problems, meaninglessness	35(21-25)	II 38
Kangaroo Legs	stillness, leap, terror	37(13-18)	II 39-40
The Distant Flash	darkness, dread, Don Juan, sensuousness	128(17)-129(4)	II 121
Skimming the Stone	dance, depth, Don Juan	129(5-8)	II 121
The Thief and the Judge	aesthetic, religious, ethical	143(35)-144(3)	II 135
The Prisoner in the Dungeon	reflection, grief, monotony, enclosure	168(29)-169(17)	II 158
The Second Face	hiddenness, grief, renunciation	172(33)-173(14)	II 161-62
The Protean Face of Grief	inventiveness, concealment	174(1-14)	II 162-63
The Hesitation Amid Shipwreck	indecision, deliberation, pathos	202(29-36)	II 189

Parable	Themes	Page (and line) Numbers	Danish Text
The One-person Skiff	autonomy, loneliness, despair	85(22)-86(11)	III 82-83
The Conqueror and the Possessor	conquest, humility, contentment	133(33)-134(27)	III 125
The Slayer of Five Wild Boars—Or Was it Four?	internal history, poet, romanticism	136(33)-137(11)	III 127-28
The Hero and the Cross Bearer	patience, moment, art, courage	138(11-35)	III 128-29
The Giant and the Cottager	appetite, satisfaction, petition	156(13-25)	III 146
Playing the Music Backwards	mistakes, retracking, demonic	168(38)-169(8)	III 158
The Count and the Countess	age, love, beauty, enjoyment	185(31)-186(34)	III 173-74
The Pleasures of Nero	hedonism, cruelty, spirit, dread	188(38)-192(37)	III 176-80
The Quiescent Sword	use, disuse, attack	223(37)-224(5)	III 207
The Aesthetic's Garden	aesthetic, ethical, immediacy	229(32)-230(20)	III 209
The Grocer's Clerk	theatre, ethical, good, bad	232(26-35)	III 215-16
The Gambler	addiction, change, moods, continuity	235(5-20)	III 218-19
The Village of Mol	learning, duty, casuistry	271(2-11)	III 251
The First Ten Lines of Balle's "Lesson-Book"	ethical, earnestness, assignment	271(14)-272(7)	III 251-52
The Ninny Who Learned	ability, development, intelligence	272(18-26)	III 252-53
Third in the Class	single duty, impression, earnestness	272(27)-274(4)	III 253-54
The Obituary Notice	pathos, immortality, proof	284(5-25)	III 265-66
The Elderly Woman at Worship	prayer, congregation, intercession	318(35)-319(32)	III 299-300
The Friendless Wise Man	friendship, devil, laughter, alone	325(33)-326(17)	III 305-06

Parable	Themes	Page (and line) Numbers	Danish Text

JOHANNES CLIMACUS OR DE OMNIBUS DUBITANDUM EST, AND A SERMON (Danish references to *Papirer*) (*Johannes Climacus eller De omnibus dubitandum est*, 1842-43, *Demis-Prædiken*, 1844)

Parable	Themes	Page (and line) Numbers	Danish Text
The Pile of Inferences	logic, balance, excess	104(19-25)	IV B 1
The Imaginary Walk	father, description, creativity, imagination	104(1)-106(5)	IV B 1
The Flight of Wild Geese	eternal philosophy, elevation	131(26-30)	IV B 1
The Doubly Fatal Sword	philosophy, doubt, beginning	138(5-22)	IV B 1
The Difference Between Seamen and Philosophers	danger, experience, adventure, doubt	143(1)-144(19)	IV B 1
The Child in Armor	imitation, apostolicity, militancy	163(29-31)	*Pap.* IV B 1
The Visit of the King	imagination, incarnation, offense	166(31)-167(27)	*Pap.* IV B 1
The Impossible Remittance	debt, impossibility, guilt, conscience	172(24)-173(2)	*Pap.* IV B 1

EDIFYING DISCOURSES, VOLUMES I-IV
(*Atten Opbyggelige Taler*, 1843-44)

I

Parable	Themes	Page (and line) Numbers	Danish Text
The Gaze of the Sailor	future, danger, faithfulness	21(20-25)	IV 26
The Undisplayed Jewel	celebration, awaiting, hope	38(8-15)	IV 37
The Successful Man	unawareness, prosperity	104(22)-105(8)	IV 86-87

II

Parable	Themes	Page (and line) Numbers	Danish Text
The Gold Ring	equality, sobriety	46(2-19)	IV 130-31
The Patient Traveler	patience, acquiescence, desire	69(7)-70(5)	IV 146-47

III

Parable	Themes	Page (and line) Numbers	Danish Text
The Wandering King	patience, tomorrow, salvation, vigilance	31(19)-32(13)	IV 181-82
The Disturbed Pool	monotony, restoration, awakening	39(25)-40(3)	IV 186-87

Parable	Themes	Page (and line) Numbers	Danish Text
The Patience of Anna	expectation, faith, fulfillment, prayer, service	41(29)-63(4)	IV 188-202
The Picture on the Cottage Wall	equality, inequality, conscience	73(14-26)	IV 212
The Straw and the Proof	existence of God, proof, youth, age	84(18-32)	IV 220
The Infirm Pensioner	eternal happiness, the age	97(12-16)	IV 228
The Stumble	rejection, eternal happiness, harmony	116(2)-117(9)	IV 241-42
The Letter and the Word	pointing, self, significance	122(14-21)	IV 246
IV			
The Banquet Invitation	contentment, language, gift, kingdom	12(18)-13(17)	IV 268-69
The Death-hour Discovery	friendship, love, misfortune, separation	26(19-30)	IV 276
The Hunter	devotion, rest, terror, edification	70(30)-71(7)	IV 304-05
The Invitation to Combat	prayer, loss, heart, victory	113(22)-115(14)	IV 332-33
The Drawing	hiddenness, artistry	140(33)-141(13)	IV 350
The Quiet Sea	reflection, power, nothingness	142(8-12)	IV 351
The Debt of Honor	prayer, providence, God	143(1-12)	IV 351

FEAR AND TREMBLING
(*Frygt og Bæven*, by Johannes de Silentio, 1843)

The Clearance Sale	ideas, modernity, speculation	22(1-4)	V 9
The Gardener's Advertisement	authorship, the age, esteem	24(8-23)	V 11
The Fifty Word Sentence	scribe, inflexibility, arbitrariness	24(23-35)	V 11
The Blackened Breast	weaning, love, negation	28(1-7)	V 14-15
He Who Works Gets the Bread	divine order, spirit, birth	38(1-27)	V 27
The Sleepless One	earnestness, Abraham, knowledge	38(33)-40(12)	V 27-29

Parable	Themes	Page (and line) Numbers	Danish Text
The World and the Parson's Preaching	philosophy, preaching, life, sense	40n	V 29n
The Swimming Belt	faith, infinity, finiteness, movement	48(29-39)	V 36
The Knight of Faith	faith, delight, interest, absurd, infinity, finiteness	49(6)-51(28)	V 36-39
The Leaping Dancer	elevation, finiteness, movement	51(31)-52(14)	V 39
The Poor Man in the Palace	humility, confidence, propriety	74(23)-75(16)	V 59-60
The Theatre of Manikins	isolation, knight of faith, paradox	89(29)-90(21)	V 73
The Bald Lover	concealment, comedy, admission, hypocrisy	94(7-26)	V 77
The Death-warrant for Essex	heroism, poetry, self-reproof	103(14-26)	V 86
Agnes and the Merman	demonic, repentance, hiddenness, revealedness	103(27)-108(21)	V 86-90
Pegging Up the Price	rigor, necessary delusion	129(27)-130(2)	V 108-09
The Stretched-out Game	imagination, play, children	131(9-17)	V 110

REPETITION
(*Gjentagelsen,* by Constantine Constantius, 1843)

Parable	Themes	Page (and line) Numbers	Danish Text
The Deaf Courtier	repetition, significance	36(1-11)	V 132
The Carriage to Berlin	intimacy, crowd, discomfort	36(19)-37(3)	V 132
The Betrothed German	language, Lent, marriage, aesthetics, repetition	39(8)-40(18)	V 133-34
The Robber Chieftain	fantasy, imagination, theatre, farce	45(25)-46(20)	V 137-38
The Division of Mankind	classification, speculation	66(7-18)	V 147
The Accident	leaving, returning, home	71(25)-72(4)	V 150
The Baby in the Perambulator	danger, tranquility	73(15)-74(11)	V 151
The Post-horn	repetition, sameness	78(9-23)	V 153
The Excavation	immobility, repetition	82(17-23)	V 155-56

154

Parable	Themes	Page (and line) Numbers	Danish Text

PHILOSOPHICAL FRAGMENTS
(*Philosophiske Smuler*, by Johannes Climacus, ed. S. K., 1844)

Parable	Themes	Page (and line) Numbers	Danish Text
The Fire-engines of Frederica	pretension, journalism, comedy	5(14-25)	VI 10-11
The Book and the Toy	decision, sin, bondage, predicament	20n	VI 21n
The Invention of Gunpowder	authorship, invention, reversal	26(23-29)	VI 25
The Road to London	God, knowability, ignorance, paradox	79n	VI 60n
The Imperial Marriage-feast	report, accessibility, contemporary	82(9)-83(14)	VI 62-63
The Holy Land Expedition	contemporaneousness, jest, fantasy	87(8)-88(18)	VI 65-66
The Appearance of the Star	elusiveness, sensation, history	100(20-31)	VI 74
The Two Sisters	quantity, quality, variety, thought	123(20-27)	VI 89
The Army Marching Backwards	triumph, mockery, faith, comedy	135(23)-136(14)	VI 97

THE CONCEPT OF DREAD
(*Begrebet Angest*, by Vigilius Haufniensis, ed. S. K., 1844)

Parable	Themes	Page (and line) Numbers	Danish Text
A Sabbatical Year for Language	ambiguity, language, thought	11(18-35)	VI 111
The Spare Diet of Psychology	ascetic, science, empiricism	20(30-32)	VI 120
The Candidacy of Trop	first sin, quantitative determination	28(15)-29(1)	VI 126-27
The Psychiatrist	self-image, wisdom, craziness, healing	48(37)-49(2)	VI 146-47
The Tightrope Dancer	psychological observer, experience, detective, empathy	49(18-38)	VI 147
The Sleeping Venus	spirit, woman, beauty	59(2-12)	VI 156-57
The Alehouse Keeper	the majority, ethics, sexuality	61(5-8)	VI 158
The Conveyance to Deer Park	speculation, beginning, indifference	76(1-11)	VI 173

Parable	Themes	Page (and line) Numbers	Danish Text
The 70,000 Years	time, space, reflection, vanishing	77(10-14)	VI 174
The Unpunctuated Treatise	traditionalism, comedy, monotony	84(10-19)	VI 181
The Talking Machine	routine, spiritlessness, politics	85(10-14)	VI 182
The Omen	fate, Napoleon, favorable conditions, battle	89(13-33)	VI 186
The Fateful Report	fate, invincibility, collapse, genius	89(38)-90(8)	VI 186-87
The Inhabitants of the Faroe Islands	joy, contributions, language, forgetfulness	91(4-11)	VI 188
The Distribution of Gifts	good and evil, choice, universal	95n	VI 191n
The Path to Perfection	narrowness, comfort, danger	104(22-27)	VI 201
The Inquisition	brain-washing, silence, shut-upness	111(14-33)	VI 208
The Candidate for Grocer's Clerk	universal history, expertise, irony	120(15-21)	VI 216-17
The Misplaced Notebooks	philosophy, immortality, forgetfulness	124(37)-125(2)	VI 221
The Bowlegged Dancing Master	congruence, saint, phoniness, the religious	125(36)-126(7)	VI 222
The Anxious King	God, uncertainty, proof	134n	VI 230n
The Pupil of Possibility	experience, awareness, education	143(4-9)	VI 238

THOUGHTS ON CRUCIAL SITUATIONS IN HUMAN LIFE
(*Tre Taler ved tænkte Leiligheder*, 1845)

Parable	Themes	Page (and line) Numbers	Danish Text
The Judgmental Buffoon	aloneness, theatrics, sin	24(29)-25(24)	VI 262-63
The Lover and the Rabble	simplicity, comparison, solitude	28(27)-29(6)	VI 265
The Loan Association	marriage, help, God, difficulty	72(27)-73(2)	VI 294
The Inconspicuous Man	death, remembrance, earnestness	75(1)-78(17)	VI 296-98
The New Year's Dream	death, wisdom, externality, earnestness	81(32)-82(16)	VI 300-01

Parable	Themes	Page (and line) Numbers	Danish Text
The Graveside Visit	refreshment, contradiction, remembrance	82(24)-83(22)	VI 301
The Single Pronouncement	death, decisiveness, earnestness, stillness	84(22)-85(16)	VI 302-03

STAGES ON LIFE'S WAY
(*Stadier paa Livets Vej*, ed. Hilarius Bogbinder, 1845)

Parable	Themes	Page (and line) Numbers	Danish Text
Drawing a Check on Eternity	recollection, remembrance	28(32-37)	VII 16-17
The Talkative Man and the Silent Man	recollection, silence, breakthrough	29(11-29)	VII 17
The Homing Dove	return, recollection, solitude	30(12-19)	VII 18
The Nook of Eight Paths	possibility, solitude, silence, ecstacy	33(22)-34(36)	VII 21-22
The Tiresome Christmas Tree	imagination, weariness, boredom	42(28-31)	VII 29
Lalage	love, loveable, universal, comic	48(35)-49(34)	VII 35-36
The Fox Trap Signs	love, warning, avoidance, vulnerability	52(1-15)	VII 38
The Pope's Cough	comic, incongruity, contradiction	54(39)-55(4)	VII 41
The Cold Shower	contradiction, comedy, love	56(4-16)	VII 42
Xanthippe *in flagrante*	jealousy, fidelity, comedy	63(5-23)	VII 49
The Deceased First Love	separation, love, comedy, dread	66(30)-67(8)	VII 53
Madam Petersen	woman, turning-points, exaggeration	69(18-26)	VII 55
A New Proof for Immortality	ideality, remarriage, obituary, woman	71(18-32)	VII 57-58
The Meat of the Turtle	marriage, complexity, unity	74(12-37)	VII 60-61
The Arbiter of Fashion	gullibility, compliance, woman, naïveté	76(3)-80(41)	VII 62-67
The Strolling Musician	marriage, single-mindedness	102(34)-103(10)	VII 89
The Spook	probability, resolution, marriage	114(26)-115(12)	VII 100

Parable	Themes	Page (and line) Numbers	Danish Text
The Difficulties of Marriage	mourning, marriage, worry, realism	119(11-27)	VII 104
He Who Loves Risks	heroism, marriage, risk, courage	120(8-34)	VII 105-06
The Tradesman's Door	resolution, marriage, constant	121(21-27)	VII 106-07
The Forlorn Valkyrie	reflection, loss of immediacy, hiddenness	123(24)-124(12)	VII 109
The Soap Made of Flint	proof, woman, praise, marriage	128(34)-129(36)	VII 114-15
The Advertisement for the Removal of Corns	certainty, tactlessness, love	130(34)-131(33)	VII 116-17
The Honest Accountant	marriage, remembrance, reliability	132(30)-133(2)	VII 118
Mother and Child at Church	concentration, prayer, love	139(37)-140(31)	VII 125-26
The Gauntlet and the Sparrow	strength, omnipotence	144(7-10)	VII 130
The Schoolmaster	gallantry, woman, irony, mockery	145(11-33)	VII 131
A New Mark on the Rafter	indebtedness, wealth, poverty	186(1-4)	VIII 17
The Soldier of the Advanced Guard	marriage, melancholy, duty	188(21-28)	VIII 19
The Child on the Esplanade	self-discipline, adaptability, melancholy, deception	188(29)-189(3)	VIII 19
The Desperate Man	conscience, duty, honor, murder	190(13-20)	VIII 21
The Second Rate Pastry Shop	attention, love, deception	194(29)-196(30)	VIII 26-28
The Woodchopper	resolution, time, mankind, instant	198(25)-199(2)	VIII 30
The Rusty Hinges	self-disclosure, silence, disinterest	200(18-30)	VIII 32
The Supple Athlete	possibility, selfhood, power	200(37)-201(3)	VIII 32-33
The Tightrope Dancers	parenting, possibility	203(32-35)	VIII 35
Rachel's Lament	aspiration, attainment, disappointment	205(1-4)	VIII 37

Parable	Themes	Page (and line) Numbers	Danish Text
The Night Watchman	alertness, silence	291(23-27)	VIII 125
The Children of Pericles	inconsistency, reversal, law	294(24-32)	VIII 128
The Woman Who Got Up By Herself	independence, autonomy, self-confidence	297(18-21)	VIII 131
The Other Coat	expressions of love, second face	310(4-15)	VIII 135
The Friendly Robber	friendly talk, embarrassment	311(7-13)	VIII 145
The Bear and the Fly	reserve, stillness, comedy, torment	328(30)-329(5)	VIII 163-64
The Peat Fosse	attentiveness, solitude, nature	333(14-35)	VIII 168-69
The Woman Who Feared Being Buried Alive	precaution, finitude, counseling	343(38)-344(14)	VIII 170
The Peril of the Sailor	patience, rescue, escape, city, solitude	346(10-33)	VIII 171
The Messenger	melancholy, permission, illusion, death, endurance	347(16)-348(3)	VIII 183
The Mussel	openness, shutness, suffering	354(15-22)	VIII 190
The Five-hundred-pound Note	sympathy, consolation, exchange	354(32)-355(3)	VIII 190-91
The Wide Horizon	eternity, nothingness, seeing	356(1-11)	VIII 192
The Prince Who Sent Back a King's Daughter	rejection, marriage, guilt	358(38)-359(1)	VIII 195
The Error that Surpassed the Text	significance, irony, arbitrariness	361(31)-362(2)	VIII 198
The Diary of Louis XVI	nothing, contents, emptiness	362(3-8)	VIII 198
Quixote's Confession	unhappy love, test, the age, illness	366(20-37)	VIII 202-03
The Protracted Creak	comedy, time, disturbance	381(18-24)	VIII 218
The Swimming Instruction	theory, existence, oratory	401(19-25)	VIII 238
The Man Who Could Talk About Everything	religious oratory, perfectability, sermon, self-concern	419(20-26)	VIII 256

Parable	Themes	Page (and line) Numbers	Danish Text
The Advice to God	self-torment, busybodies, fixed idea	420(32)-421(16)	VIII 258
The Swift Ride of the King	solitude, company, authorship	473(1-10)	VIII 274
The Most Dangerous Seducer	ideality, imagination, deception	442(25)-443(15)	VIII 279
The Eel's Punishment	authorship, pleasure, injury	444(30-33)	VIII 281

CONCLUDING UNSCIENTIFIC POSTSCRIPT
(*Afsluttende uvidenskabelig Efterskrift*, by Johannes Climacus, ed. S. K., 1846)

The Welcome of the Incognito Hero	reception, literary success, expectancy, enthusiasm	3(13)-4(12)	IX 9-10
The Torchlight Procession	obligation, approval, negation	4(32)-5(7)	IX 10-11
The Embarrassed Lover	proof, faith, shame	31(27-35)	IX 30
The Man Who Was Not Sure He Was a Christian	anger, Christendom, conformity	49(16-34)	IX 47
The Flute-player	philosophy, philosopher, existence	50(30-32)	IX 48
Sawing Wood	lightness, speculation, subjectivity	55(21-28)	IX 52
The Poor Lodger	admiration, subjectivity, G. E. Lessing	59(1)-61(31)	IX 55-57
The Way Station	admiration, world-history, G. E. Lessing	63(22-33)	IX 59
Hegel's Dying Words	direct communication, misunderstanding	65n-66n	IX 61n
The Maiden Who Needed Assurance	communication, double reflection	68n	IX 64n
The Guest Hit by a Roof Tile	uncertainty, comedy, exception	80(1)-81(23)	IX 74n
The Gaze of Socrates	prayer, petition, silence	83n	IX 77n
The Easy Guillotine	death, simplicity	94(10-17)	IX 88
Kneeling Before the System	postponement, unfinished system	97(36)-98(11)	IX 91-92
The Lost Silk Umbrella	truth, advertising, system	99(6-14)	IX 93

Parable	Themes	Page (and line) Numbers	Danish Text
The Ambitious Dancer	infinitude, leap, moment	112(36-39)	IX 106
The Royal "We"	speculation, oaths, game	113(7-23)	IX 106
The Wonderful Lamp	freedom, servant, God	124(8-13)	IX 115
The World-historical Swashbuckler	prophecy, nineteenth century, comedy	129(17-39)	IX 119-20
The Bellows-blower	oratory, applause, solitude, speaking	130(31)-131(9)	IX 121
The Ill-clad Socrates	self-awareness, world-historical, ethical	131n-132n	IX 122n
The Difficulty of Playing Hamlet	prayer, disturbance, Luther	145(21-31)	IX 135-36
The Christmas Tree and the Bramble	system, celebration, sarcasm	145(35)-146(4)	IX 136
The Table Pounder	death, objective speech, deception	151(34)-152(15)	IX 141-42
The Danish History Examination	subjectivity, immortality, learning	154(16-37)	IX 144
The Armor of Mars	immortality, self-contradiction, system	155(26-34)	IX 145
The Thankful Man	prayer, simplicity, humor, difficulty	159(14)-160(3)	IX 149
The Promise to Meet Again	eternity, woe, clergy, forgetting	163(14-21)	IX 153
The Conversion of Dr. Hartspring	Hegelianism, miracle, sign	163(34-39)	IX 153
The Vomitive	purgation, repentance	166(25-30)	IX 156
The Tenant and the Owner	speculation, faith, mystery, paradox	192(12-26)	IX 179
The Fullness of Time	paradox, Privatdocent, professors	198(4-11)	IX 184
The Battle of Zama	faith, seeing, paradox, understanding	201n, 202n	IX 187n
The Aged Parent Who Was Declared Incompetent	renewal, ingratitude, Christianity	208(6-15)	IX 193
The Garden of the Dead	promise, faith, oath, forget, inwardness	210(20)-216(35)	IX 196-202
The Large Green Bird	revelation, attention, direct relation	219(18-24)	IX 204

162

Parable	Themes	Page (and line) Numbers	Danish Text
The Man Six Yards Tall	deceive, seeing, revelation, direct	220(8-14)	IX 205
The Prolific Author	nature, astonishment, revelation	220(35)-221(12)	IX 206
The Dilettante	knowledge, inwardness, communication	232(1-20)	IX 217
The King and the Minister	secrecy, genius, God, shrewdness	233n	IX 218n
The Man Standing on One Leg	communication, experiment	235(37)-236(6)	IX 220-21
The Full Mouth	communication, deprivation	245n	IX 229n
The Ten Thousand Adherents	indirect communication, conversion	247(38)-248(11)	IX 233
The Harvest	comedy, sensitivity, immediacy, authority, care	250(38)-251(17)	IX 236
The Sailor Who Fell From the Mast	recollection, repetition, venture	253(9-19)	IX 238-39
Valborg Revisited	repetition, Shakespeare, inwardness	254n	IX 239n
The Lacemaker	slavery, impersonal, thinker	268(25-37)	X 10
The Epigram for Hegel	misunderstand, doubt, existence, pure thought	275(17-36)	X 17
Socrates and Hegel	system, understanding, human being	276(5-10)	X 17-18
The Pegasus and the Worn-out Jade	passion, thinker, eternity, time	276(19-39)	X 18
The Hermit	pure thought, unreality, comedy, forgetfulness	283(28)-284(5)	X 25-26
The Announcement of Misprints	fraud, departure, waiting	291(18)-292(6)	X 31-32
Blowing Up the World With a Syllogism	thought, existence	296(1-7)	X 35-36
The Letter from Heaven	anonymity, Hegel, pure thought	296(26)-297(29)	X 36-37
The Levite	thinking, intention, action, good	303(17)-304(2)	X 42-43

163

Parable	Themes	Page (and line) Numbers	Danish Text
The Glorious Deed of Dion	external decision, internal, deed	304(27)-305(9)	X 43-44
The Domino-player	system, knowing, ceasing to live, shadow, war, diplomacy	307(23)-308(15)	X 46-47
The One-sided Individual	fashion, intellect, ethical, forgetfulness, present age	312(1-28)	X 50-51
The Court Jester	moment, intervals, lifetime, wit	314(25-30)	X 53
The Game of Idealism	existence, lecture, satire, comedy, imagination, professor	315(19)-316(2)	X 54
Napoleon at the Pyramids	heroism, challenge, masses, cowardice	318(7-21)	X 56
The Insomnia of Themistocles	reality, possibility, ethical, ideal	321(36)-322(8)	X 59
Shrimps, Greens, and Oysters	confusion, Christianity, speculation	324(18-25)	X 61
The Toothless Old Man	Christianity, emasculation, language	325(11-14)	X 62
The Obsequious Transformation of the King	revolution, prisoner, servant, Christianity, costume	325(31-39)	X 62
The Inspection	resignation, mediation, constant	354(29)-355(6)	X 89-90
The Luckless Officer of Napoleon's Army	result, greatness, fate, success	356(13)-357(31)	X 91-92
The Two Ways	pleasure, virtue	361(3-29)	X 95-96
The Backward Pupil	renunciation, finishing, task, patience	363(27-39)	X 98
The Stranger	resignation, absolute telos, finite	367(26)-368(9)	X 102
The Woman in Love	monasticism, merit, humility	371(12-36)	X 105-06
Physician's Program for a New Asylum	cloister, holy man, inwardness	372(14)-373(3)	X 106-07
The Embarrassed Parishioner	human beings, glory, idealization	374(9-21)	X 108
The Run Toward the Leap	certainty, venture, seriousness	380(9-15)	X 114

Parable	Themes	Page (and line) Numbers	Danish Text
The Immobilized Carriage	religiousness, elevation, poetic, comic	393(17-34)	X 126
The Comic Clergyman in a Tragedy	pretension, pathos, theatre, poetic	395n	X 127n
The Cry for a New Body	suffering, expression, pathos, reality, accidental, religiousness	398(13-32)	X 131
The Acclaimed Actor	applause, thanks, ambiguity, rebellion	399n	X 132n
The New Bell Pull	humor, suffering, misfortune	401(9-30)	X 133-34
The Brother of Aristocratic Acquaintances	intensity, strenuousness, God, humor	402(20-35)	X 135
The Postponed Auction	haste, contradiction, humor, urgency	402(36)-403(8)	X 135
The Doctor's Diagnosis	riddle, existence, illness	403(9-33)	X 135-36
The Living Room and the Church	ordinariness, religious oratory	415(13)-416(26)	X 147-48
The Spy	the age, religiosity, outing, Sunday, weekdays, investigation, clergy	417(22)-431(12)	X 149-62
The Confinement	conception of God, finitude, mutuality	432(14-33)	X 163-64
The God Who Fell in Love with an Earthly Woman	ignorance, knowledge, anxiety, unhappiness	438(8-19)	X 169
The Workman and the Princess	humility, love, work	441(6-19)	X 172
Wednesday in the Deer Park	religious consciousness, inwardness, immediacy, suffering, humor, God	442(3)-447(10)	X 173-78
Swearing by the Fire Tongs	comedy, contradiction, finite, freedom	459n-462n	X 189n-93n
Icarus	ideal, progress, retrogression, ethical	469(27-32)	X 200
The Leader of the Army of India	thought, existence	470(2-13)	X 201
The Penance	satisfaction, guilt, hope, appeasement	483(8-39)	X 214

Parable	Themes	Page (and line) Numbers	Danish Text
The Licking	happiness, penance, irony, humor	490(15-26)	X 221
The Sinking Ship	contradiction, comedy, activity	493(13-18)	X 224
The Presumptuous Man and the Believer	belief against understanding, comic	503(1)-504(17)	X 234-36
The Second-hand Report	assurance, love, witnesses	511(14-21)	X 243
The Deposit in the Burial Society	sincerity, lukewarmness, death	521(22-31)	X 253-54
The Man Converted on New Year's Eve	information, communication, conversion	542(21)-543(24)	X 275-76
The Robber's Wig	recognition, oath, incognito	544(6-22)	X 277

THE PRESENT AGE
(*En literair Anmeldelse, To Tidsaldre*, 1846)

Parable	Themes	Page (and line) Numbers	Danish Text
The Impending Revolution	deliberation, impression, postponement	34(31)-35(16)	XIV 64-65
The Banquet	applause, admiration, extraordinary	37(28)-38(24)	XIV 67
The Manufacture of Wit	mystery, transformation, necessity	40(18-28)	XIV 69
The Street Fight	the crowd, humor, contradiction, leveling	54(25)-55(18)	XIV 79-80
The Gallery	press, mass, gossip, superiority	64(25)-65(10)	XIV 86
The End of Gossip	talkativeness, law, trivia	71(23)-72(14)	XIV 96
The Phrase-book for Lovers	abstraction, education	77(18-26)	XIV 95

ON AUTHORITY AND REVELATION, THE BOOK ON ADLER (Danish references to *Papirer*)
(*Bogen om Adler*, 1846-47)

Parable	Themes	Page (and line) Numbers	Danish Text
The Dangerous Boiler	danger, authors, ambitiousness	6(22-25)	VII² B 235
The Outcry	the age, writers, romanticism	6(35)-7(17)	VII² B 235
The Physician and the Sick Man	authority, disease, author	11(9-20)	VII² B 235

Parable	Themes	Page (and line) Numbers	Danish Text
The Elaborate Answer	revelation, genius, Paul, brevity	15(14-26)	VII² B 235
The Prince's Exercise	Denmark, authors	18(12-18)	VII² B 235
The Army vs. the Establishment	extraordinary, the public	21(10-27)	VII² B 235
The Establishment's Revolutionary Teacher	revolution, responsibility, cowardice	28(28)-29(26)	VII² B 235
The Digestive Disturbance	marriage, reflection, spiritual life	29(34)-30(9)	VII² B 235
The Dunce	concreteness, particularity, learning	31(16)-32(10)	VII² B 235
The Modern Martyr	security, risk, reform	33(22-27)	VII² B 235
The "Movement" Personality	reformer, huckster, politics	41(30)-42(15)	VII² B 235
The Head of the Movement	reform, leadership, pretensions	44(16-32)	VII² B 235
The Draw of the Ship	profundity, externality, inwardness	47(32)-48(20)	VII² B 235
The Patience of Mary	time, faith, humility, birth	50n	VII² B 235
The Hellstone	harm, established order, sacrifice	51(6-16)	VII² B 235
The Tollclerk	arrogance, consequences, order	55(34)-56(3)	VII² B 235
The Author Who Published Four Books at Once	authorship, ambition, pretenses	94(10-19)	VII² B 235
The King's Command	authority, genius, apostolicity, revelation, obedience	108(21)-110(6)	VII² B 235
The Clever Decree	authority, obedience	113(13-28)	VII² B 235
Declining a Paradigm	understanding, repetition	124(25)-125(6)	VII² B 235
The Dizzy Coachman	dizziness, indefiniteness, limitation	127(32)-128(31)	VII² B 235
The Formula	magic, repetition, profundity	136(7-35)	VII² B 235

Parable	Themes	Page (and line) Numbers	Danish Text
The Lottery	conjurer, abruptness, scenario	137(24)-138(2)	VII² B 235
The Frenetic Preacher	conviction, collusion, proof	151(20)-152(1)	VII² B 235
Archimedes' Discovery	nakedness, excuse, offense, prudery	162(25-32)	VII² B 235
The Merchant Bearend	philistinism, mistake, offense	163(3-7)	VII² B 235
"Next Time"	examination, adage, postponement	172(6-10)	VII² B 235
The Whispered Yes	confirmation, wedding, seriousness, religious instruction, decisiveness	181(3)-186(8)	VII² B 235
The Oversized Garment	upbringing, growth, parenting	187(8-13)	VII² B 235
The Love From Earliest Childhood	self-deception, poetized truth	190(34)-191(8)	VII² B 235

PURITY OF HEART
(*Opbyggelige Taler i forskjellig Aand*, Pt. 1, "En Leiligheds-Tale," 1847)

Parable	Themes	Page (and line) Numbers	Danish Text
The Fugitive	guilt, repentance, forgetfulness	44(34)-45(23)	XI 24-25
The Changing of Raiment for a Feast	confession, silence, manyness	47(12)-49(15)	XI 26-27
The Brook	confession, stillness, preparation	49(16)-50(3)	XI 27-28
The Last Bubble of the Drowning Man	desperation, hope	64(25)-65(27)	XI 37-38
The Girl with Money	love, deception, influence	70(28)-71(19)	XI 41-42
The Fear of Medicine	double-mindedness, imagination, sickness, punishment, anxiety	70(16)-82(22)	XI 47-49
Teaching the Child to Walk	fear, encouragement, double-mindedness	85(4)-86(10)	XI 51-52
The Unused Mirror	business, excuses, self-knowledge	108(19-32)	XI 66
The Man Who Did Wrong in Order to Obtain His Right	double-mindedness, justice, suffering	112(15)-113(7)	XI 69

Parable	Themes	Page (and line) Numbers	Danish Text
The Freight Barge	will, conflict, double-mindedness	117(24)-118(12)	XI 73
The Battleship and the Sloop	risk, willingness, knowing in advance	129(17-23)	XI 81
The Thinker and the Follower	originality, misunderstanding, speech	136(15-24)	XI 85-86
The False Tone	empathy, eternity, self-deception	141(18-23)	XI 89
The Mirror of Heaven	purity of heart, sea, yearning, calm	176(10)-177(9)	XI 112
The Schoolboy's Fearlessness	crowd, ridicule, fear, father	196(12-26)	XI 125
The Aim and the Spot	means, ends, goal, accident	202(34)-203(13)	XI 129
The King, The Beggar, and the Alter Ego	universality, equality, unity, clannishness	206(7)-207(2)	XI 131-32
Eternity's Question	faith, suffering, change, status	209(1)-210(15)	XI 133-34

THE GOSPEL OF SUFFERING *and* THE LILIES OF THE FIELD
(*Opbyggelige Taler i forskjellig Aand*, Pt. 3, "Lidelsernes Evangelium," Pt. 2, "Lilerne paa Marken og Himlens Fugle," 1847)

The Imperiled Lovers	lightness, burden	26(6-20)	XI 218
The Feather and the Great Weight	joy, strength, faith	30(5-14)	XI 221
The Hopeless Maiden	impossibility, faith	30(15)-31(6)	XI 221
The Wise Virgins	certainty, faith	31(7-14)	XI 221
The Meek Slave	meekness, slavery, affirmation	38(26)-39(2)	XI 226-27
The Woman Who Became Younger	penance, age, youth	62(25)-63(10)	XI 243
What Holds the Ship Together	shipwreck, faith, disintegration	72(3-32)	XI 250
The Overtaxed Horse	despair, burden, hopelessness	80(17)-81(10)	XI 255-56
The Competent Driver	concentration, focus, waste	105(3-26)	XI 272-73
The Envy of the Wayfarer	affliction, the way	108(28)-109(9)	XI 275

Parable	Themes	Page (and line) Numbers	Danish Text
The Lights that Obscure the Stars	perspective, suffering, light	123(4-13)	XI 285
The Language of the Court	afflictions, love, eternity	130(26)-132(6)	XI 290-91
The Loyal Courtier	fidelity, service, unchanging	133(9-16)	XI 292
The Pound of Feathers	the temporal, suffering, happiness	134(12-28)	XI 293
The Imaginative Youth	ideals, imagination, suffering	147(9)-149(13)	XI 301-02
The Roaring Fire	defeat, conviction, fire	163(27)-164(4)	XI 312
The Magnifying Glass	human achievement, nature	175(7-17)	XI 151
The Lily and the Troubled One	trust, providence, humanity	176(1-29)	XI 152
The Liberation of the Lily	boredom, comparison, care	178(26)-181(7)	XI 154-55
Solomon and Lazarus	human, address, distinction	183(19-31)	XI 157
Birdwatching	attention, concentration, human	184(28)-185(32)	XI 158-59
The Field Birds	anxiety, trust, feeding	186(6-16)	XI 159
The Stock Dove	envy, uncertainty, anxiety, self-rejection	188(9)-191(4)	XI 161-62
The Inquisitive Maiden	concern, serenity, anxiety, thanks	195(24)-196(2)	XI 165-66
The Medicine Chest	anxiety, hypocrisy, contradiction	197(5-10)	XI 166
The Fireworks Display	boredom, time, diversion, eternity	201(14)-203(2)	XI 169-70
The Physician's Voice	death, severity, mildness	225(27)-226(6)	XI 186
The Maiden's Choice	choice, love	228(15-21)	XI 188
The Smallest Coin	humility, image of God	234(14-16)	XI 192
The Things Left Behind	kingdom of God, fortune, happiness	236(5-15)	XI 193-94

WORKS OF LOVE
(*Kjerlighedens Gjerninger*, 1847)

The Flowing Wellspring	hiddenness, love, eternal	27(32)-28(4)	XII 15-16

Parable	Themes	Page (and line) Numbers	Danish Text
Sterling Silver	love, duty, continuity, test	47(14-35)	XII 37
The Vampire	habit, sleep, lukewarmness	50(37)-51(11)	XII 41-42
The Thunder of a Hundred Cannon	habit, reinforcement, hearing	51(31-40)	XII 42
The Coopersmith's Kettle	distance, neighbor, hearing	88(25-31)	XII 81
The Banquet Feast	equality, the poor, festivity	90(32)-91(32)	XII 83-84
The Yes Man	honor, haste, promise, deception, detour, straightforwardness	100(1)-101(27)	XII 93-95
The Artist's Sketch	law, love, indefiniteness, completion	110(26)-111(7)	XII 105
The Seven and the Seven Others	irresponsibility, denial, referral	121(3-26)	XII 116-17
The World's Love	limited, "to a certain degree," good and evil, rejection	126(20)-127(22)	XII 122-23
The Terminal Case	endurance, perseverance, demand, continuing	134(35)-135(18)	XII 131
The Scrubwoman	conscience, change, inwardness, quietness, equality, status	137(16)-138(15)	XII 133-34
The Bound Heart	infinite obligation, commitment, freedom, pure heart	148(9-36)	XII 145
The Friend Who Didn't Help	mob, denial, loving those we see, Peter	165(20)-167(23)	XII 163-65
The Strong-box	envy, love, loss, possession	172(8-19)	XII 171
The Bookkeeping Relationship	sacrifice, debt, calculation, finite, remaining in debt	173(31)-174(23)	XII 173
The Prince and the Simple Man	comparison, infinite, finite, love	178(28)-179(11)	XII 177-78
The Enthusiast and the Tempter	sacrifice, comparison, dizziness	179(12)-180(11)	XII 178-79
The Puzzlement of the Naughty Children	misunderstanding, world, Christian, parental standards	195(23)-196(18)	XII 197
The Experienced Horse-trainer	human differences, impetuosity, ambiguity	217(6-19)	XII 222

Parable	Themes	Page (and line) Numbers	Danish Text
The Deceiver and the True Lover	reciprocity, love, strength	226(5)-230(19)	XII 232-36
The Festival	eternity, time, moment, victory	231(1)-233(4)	XII 237-39
The Child and the Great Task	despair, hope, abandonment, lure, eternal, future	236(26)-237(6)	XII 242-43
The Courtier Who Stayed in The Background	love, independence, debt, independence	259(13-29)	XII 266-67
The Child in the Den of Thieves	understanding, evil, discovery, sins	265(38)-267(11)	XII 274-75
The Secret Love	forgiveness, silence, discovery, sins	268(35)-269(8)	XII 277
The Detective and the Lover	mitigating explanation, experience, clue, discovery, good, evil	271(14)-273(14)	XII 279-82
The Desert Spring	love abides, eternity, consolation	280(15-19)	XII 289
The Gift of Waiting	time, endurance, uncertainty	281(4-31)	XII 290
The Incomplete Sentence	covenant, breaking-point, past, future, abiding love	284(10)-285(19)	XII 293-94
The Waiting Girl	expectation, eros, eternal love, moment	287(18)-289(35)	XII 297-99
The City for Sale	money, avarice, world, teaching	296(11-28)	XII 306
The Late Sleepers	church, theatre, money, seriousness	297(4-27)	XII 307
Lazarus and the Dogs	mercy, riches, inhumanity	299(23-40)	XII 310
The Two Travelers Attacked by Thieves	prayer, mercy, disability	300(8-21)	XII 310-11
The Painter Who Tried to Portray Mercy	inexpressibility, cruelty, nothingness	300(22)-301(22)	XII 311
The Countenance of the Eternal	mercy, power, wealth, generosity	302(28-40)	XII 313
The Waterfall and the Quiet Pond	distraction, mercy, movement	303(18-28)	XII 314
The General Who Dreaded Victory	calm, exhaustion, conquering	307(9-21)	XII 318

Parable	Themes	Page (and line) Numbers	Danish Text
The Bookmark	memory, death, forgetfulness	325(16-20)	XII 337
The Proud Man and the Dead Man	forgetfulness, memory, pride	327(33)-328(6)	XII 340
The Slave's Reminder	memory, forgetfulness, jealousy	334(11-36)	XII 346
The Homeliest Man	Socrates, beauty, congruity	341(7-34)	XII 353-54
The Educator	God, mildness, rigor, love, conscience	349(2-28)	XII 359
The Arrest of the Valet	privacy, magistracy, guilt, God	352(12-29)	XII 362-63
The Accuser Who Was Arrested	authorities, fraud, privacy, God	353(3-24)	XII 363-64

CRISIS IN THE LIFE OF AN ACTRESS
(*Krisen og en Krise i en Skuespillerindes Liv*, by Inter et Inter, *Fædrelandet*, Nos. 188-91, 24-27 July, 1848)

The Actress's Gift to the Playwright	self-awareness, genius, soulfulness	77(7-11)	XIV 113
The Light Burden and the Heavy Pause	freedom, anxiety, relief	78(16-31)	XIV 114
The Daughter of the Regiment	gifted, personification, admiration, ambush	79(15-32)	XIV 115
The Daily Visit of the King	habit, unchanging, fraud	80(31)-81(4)	XIV 116

CHRISTIAN DISCOURSES, *including* THE LILIES OF THE FIELD AND THE BIRDS OF THE AIR *and* THREE DISCOURSES AT THE COMMUNION ON FRIDAYS
(*Christelige Taler*, 1848; *Lilien paa Marken og Fuglen under Himlen*, 1849; *Tre Taler ved Altergangen om Fredagen*, 1849)

The Game of "Emperor"	reality, unreality, eternal, temporal	56(16-24)	XIII 56
The "Ghost-ride"	nothingness, immobility, nightmare	56(23)-57(2)	XIII 56
The Bird and Tomorrow	anxiety, time, dreams, now	73(1-25)	XIII 71
The Dowsing-rod	edification, the dismaying, depths	102(18-23)	XIII 96

Parable	Themes	Page (and line) Numbers	Danish Text
Death as Comedian	suffering, "once," temporal illusion, acting	107(25-36)	XIII 101
The Gold in the Fire	purification, loss, bereavement	108(6-12)	XIII 101
The Cup and the Triumph	art, suffering, "once," obedience, instant, eternity	108(38)-109(25)	XIII 102-03
The Disguised Robber	affliction, hope, mask, acting, entertainment	111(1-28)	XIII 105
The Villain	affliction, hope, assault, demand	115(32)-116(16)	XIII 109-10
The Pressure Spring	hiddenness, affliction	116(17-24)	XIII 110
The Grain of Corn	hope, eternity, inwardness, affliction	116(25-32)	XIII 110
The Unused Wings	extremity, daily use, hope	116(37)-117(2)	XIII 110
The Forced Confession	pain, effort, admission, hope	117(3-15)	XIII 110-11
The Stiffnecked Witness	court, contempt, affliction	117(13-27)	XIII 111
The Jet of Water	pressure, elevation	117(34-40)	XIII 111
The Trap Door	riches, poverty, affliction	119(1-31)	XIII 112
The Labor for All	hope, decisiveness, universality	122(5-17)	XIII 115
The Precious Perfume	communication, concealment	123(18-25)	XIII 116
The Stranger's Inquiry	strife, importance, world, godly talk	129(1)-130(9)	XIII 121-22
The Artist's Perspective	eternity, distance, perspective	140(11-17)	XIII 131
The Ruinous Comfort	severity, despair, pastoral care	141(32)·142(10)	XIII 132-33
The Blind and Deaf Man	belief, loss, world, gain	152(4-29)	XIII 142
The Nettle	sting, resolution, firmness	161(33)-162(7)	XIII 151

Parable	Themes	Page (and line) Numbers	Danish Text
The Puzzled Child	crucifixion, art, curiosity, anxiety	174(23)-176(19)	XVI 168-69
The Picture of Perfection	imagination, ideal, suffering, reality, dream, endurance, governance	185(9)-194(9)	XVI 178-86
The Discovery of Gunpowder	time, result, pondering, accident	203(7-35)	XVI 194-95
The Linguist and His Disciple	foregoer, successor, way, truth	204(5-37)	XVI 195-96
The Youth Who was Prepared to Suffer All	Christianity, Christendom, self-denial, humor	208(15-35)	XVI 199-200
The Shoemaker	direct recognition, opposition, indifference	210(2-22)	XVI 201
The Picture That Looked Back	object, reflection, truth, sermon	228(24)-229(3)	XVI 218
The Man Who Declined to be Admired	imitation, imagination, heroism, withdrawal, safety, theatre	236(35)-238(18)	XVI 226-27
The Calm of the Artist	portrait, Christ, artistic indifference, actor, sacrilege	247(21)-249(10)	XVI 236-37
The Melancholy Lover	sorrow, sin, forgiveness, indifference	262(27)-264(6)	XVII 14-15

THE POINT OF VIEW FOR MY WORK AS AN AUTHOR
(*Synspunket for min Forfatter-Virksomhed*, 1848; *Om min Forsatter-Virksomhed*, 1851)

The New Year's Visitor	repentance, Christendom, costume	34(11-19)	XVIII 101
The Spy in a Higher Service	suspicion, illusions, deception	87(16)-88(1)	XVIII 134
The Reverted Fortune	revolt, Christianity, unclaimed	133(11)-134(9)	XVIII 154

FOR SELF-EXAMINATION *and* JUDGE FOR YOURSELVES! *and* THREE DISCOURSES
(*Til Selvprøvelse*, 1851; *Dommer Selv!*, 1852; *To Taler ved Altergangen om Fredagen*, 1851)

The Bellicose Youth	merit, works, faith alone, Luther	40(19-34)	XVII 60-61

Parable	Themes	Page (and line) Numbers	Danish Text
The Thirtieth Percentile	standards, Christianity, bourgeois, dilution, apathy	207(39)-209(4)	XVII 219-20
Christianhaven Cholera	worldliness, dilution, Christianity	211(6-25)	XVII 222
The Awakened Appetite	hunger, proofs, suffering	211(25-30)	XVII 222
The Wayfarer	time, eternity, change	232(23)-233(5)	XIX 259-60
The Burial Plot	promise, forgetfulness, change	236(32)-237(15)	XIX 263
The Desert Wanderer	refreshment, unchanging, God	239(21)-240(28)	XIX 265-66

ATTACK UPON "CHRISTENDOM"
(*Bladartikler* I-XXI, *Fædrelandet*, 1854-55; *Dette skal siges; saa være det sa sagt*, 1855; *Øieblikket*, 1-9, 1855; *Hvad Christus dømmer om officiel Christendom*, 1855)

Parable	Themes	Page (and line) Numbers	Danish Text
Smoking Out Illusions	incendiarism, Christendom	41(8-17)	XIX 54
The Schoolmaster's Credentials	royal commission, claims, authority	43(19-28)	XIX 57
The Signboard	honesty, witness, truth	49(1-15)	XIX 64-65
The Disposal of Town Hall	cheapness, eternal blessedness	50(24)-51(7)	XIX 67
The Whisper of Countess Orsini	concealment, revelation, comedy	68(1-17)	XIX 85
The Swoop of the Eagle	concentration, intensiveness, blow	81(16-24)	XIX 93
The Sensible Burgomaster	state, Christianity, status	102(25-31)	XIX 112-13
The Return of the Apostle	state, king, priests, renunciation	102(32)-104(6)	XIX 113-14
The Freethinker	rejection, consequence, burial, embarrassment	107(13-36)	XIX 117
The Threat	profit, comedy, Christian, self-actualization	110(10-29)	XIX 121-22
The Fellow of the Old School	strictness, shrewdness, God	113(4-11)	XIX 126

Index

Absolute, the, 53f., 96, 120ff.
actor, acting, 46ff., 77, 89, 107, 129
aesthetic, the, 4, 126, 137
anger, 23, 63, 102
anthropology, 11, 40ff., 51, 60ff., 82ff., 92
anxiety, 57, 96, 115
Aristophanes, 7
Aristotle, 16
art, artist, 39, 108, 129
Attack Upon "Christendom," 14, 49, 73
authority, 9, 30, 59, 96
authors, 5, 6, 21, 34, 69

becoming oneself, ix-xi, 19, 85
beer, 49
books, 10, 34f., 126
boredom, 8, 11, 69

Cadoux, A. T., xi
certainty, 23f., 56, 103ff., 132
change, 33, 119
charity, 36, 103ff., 121f.
child, children, 103ff., 124
choice, xii, 16, 33, 72, 120ff.
Christ, 32, 36, 134
Christendom, 49, 53ff., 87
Christian, Christianity, 55, 66, 68, 76, 90, 123
civil religion, 49, 53ff., 68, 87
comedy, 9, 30, 47. *See also* laughter
communication, 27f., 32f., 87, 135; indirect communication, vii, xii, xv-xvi, 32f., 132

Concept of Dread, The, 47, 95
Concept of Irony, The, 29
Concluding Unscientific Post-script, xii, xiv, xxi, 9, 50, 66, 85, 91, 129
conscience, 10, 37, 57, 129
contradiction, 9, 42, 125
counsel, 35, 101
Crisis in the Life of an Actress, 21f.
critics, criticism, 4, 12, 131

danger, 15, 31, 38, 58, 123
death, 38, 48, 63, 111ff.
decision, 16, 23, 32f., 120ff.
delusion, 21, 45
despair, 17, 25, 63, 87
Diogenes, 5
disciple, discipline, 23f., 33, 59
disenchantment, 20, 27, 58, 82
dog, 8, 21
double reflection, xii
dream, 26, 100, 136
drinking, drunkenness, 19, 71, 86

edification, viii, xii, 89, 128
Edifying Discourses, 12
Either/Or, viii, 3, 4, 7, 10, 11, 20, 27, 56, 58, 85, 125ff.
end of the world, 3
equality, 41ff., 48
erudition, 77ff., 90f.
eternity, 46f., 94, 101, 119
ethical, the, xiv, 15f., 34ff., 53ff., 60ff., 67, 80, 120ff., 126, 129, 134f., 137

existence, 25, 38, 76, 99

time, 3, 5, 6, 27, 37, 46, 69, 85, 94, 99
Tordenskjold, Peder, 9, 131
Training in Christianity, xiii, 33
travel, 14, 19, 39, 57, 119
truth, xii, 23, 91
tub, 5
tyranny, 4, 23, 61ff.

union, 43

wager, 15
warning, 3, 123
Western philosophy, vii

will, xiv
wisdom, wise man, 26, 37, 60, 66, 94, 124
wish, 40ff., 125
witness, 22f.
woman, 36, 40ff., 82ff., 99, 128ff., 135
Word of God, 77ff.
Works of Love, 36, 39, 48, 71, 123
world history, the world historical, 21, 129

youth, 20, 68, 72, 124